Relaxing on the beach at home in Kincasslagh during a break from touring

Opposite page right: As a tee[n]
ager, I was a member of the I[...]
Mullaghduff Fife and Drum B[...]
I carried the flag, that's how [...]
cal I was. Opposite page left: [...]
One of the early gifts I receiv[ed]
from fans was an Easter egg w[...]
playing with my first band, Th[e]
Grassroots, in 1985. Fans stil[l]
shower me with presents.

Left: Here I am, aged 15, with[...]
nie McGarvey's donkey, John[...]
Below: Posing with my moth[er]
1972.

Below: A family wedding. The bride was my sister, Kathleen, who married John Doogan. They're pictured with my brother John [extreme left], James and yours truly. Front row: Brigid [John's wife], my mother, Eileen [James's wife], Margaret and my nephew, Frankie.

Above: An early photo session. Oh, how I hated having my photo taken.

Right: Didn't I look so coy way back then?

Follow Your Dream

Daniel O' Donnell

with

EDDIE ROWLEY

THE O'BRIEN PRESS
DUBLIN

First published 1992 by The O'Brien Press Ltd.,
20 Victoria Road, Dublin 6, Ireland.

British Library Cataloguing-in-publication Data
O'Donnell, Daniel
Follow Your Dream: Daniel O'Donnell Story
I. Title
941.7082092

ISBN 0–86278–319–4

10 9 8 7 6 5 4 3 2 1

Cover Design: Michael O'Brien
Typesetting: The O'Brien Press
Separations: The City Office, Dublin
Printing: Guernsey Press, Guernsey, Channel Islands

EDDIE ROWLEY is chief showbiz writer with the top-selling Irish newspaper, the SUNDAY WORLD, which also circulates in London and New York. A respected journalist in his field, Rowley is regularly invited to interview the top names in showbiz on the world scene. His work takes him around the globe every year, meeting the major celebrities.

The galaxy of stars Rowley has featured in his weekly column reads like a Who's Who of the entertainment world; from Yoko Ono to Tom Jones, La Toya Jackson to Bryan Adams and Tammy Wynette to Garth Brooks.

The Dublin-based writer first met Daniel O' Donnell in 1991, when he began editing the singer's new weekly column in the SUNDAY WORLD. A bond of friendship was established between the two men and when Daniel decided to record his life story in book form he employed Rowley's expertise.

CONTENTS

1 *BOSCO* 9

2 *MY WONDERLAND* 14

3 *GROWING UP* 23

4 *MARGO* 35

5 *FROM THE GRAVEYARD TO THE STAGE* 54

6 *MY DONEGAL SHORE AND THE MIRACLE* 60

7 *THE SECOND COMING* 69

8 *TV AND MY IDOL* 101

9 *THOUSANDS FOR TEA* 110

10 *MY TEAM AND ON THE ROAD* 118

11 *WALKING ON WATER* 130

12 *LOST LOVE* 138

13 *OUT OF CONTROL* 143

14 *CONQUERING THE MOUNTAIN* 149

DISCOGRAPHY 155

Start spreading the news [New York, 1991].

BOSCO

☆

IF I hadn't made my name as a singer, I'd still be known at home as Daniel Bosco. Growing up, we were known as the Bosco family. That name distinguished us from the other O'Donnells living in the area. My eldest brother is called John Bosco and it was derived from his name. It's a common feature in our neck of the woods where there are numerous families bearing the same surname. Letters would arrive at our house with just the name Bosco written on the envelope. The post would reach its destination without a hitch because we were the only Boscos living in the locality.

My father, who came from Acres, near Burtonport, County Donegal, was Francie O'Donnell. But he and his family were known as the Donie Owens. I know the nick-names all sound very confusing to outsiders, but they actually worked very well. His father's name was Daniel and I'm called after my grand-father. My father's mother was Kitty Duffy, but she was known as Kitty Johnny Jondie because there were so many Duffys. She married Donie Owen and they had eleven children, my father being the second youngest and the seventh son.

Being the seventh son, he had the cure of something they called 'the evil'. It was some kind of lump that people devel-oped on their bodies and he could cure it with special prayers. He cured several neighbours in his day.

My grandfather on my mother's side was James McGonagle. And my grandmother was Margaret Sharkey, known as Mar-garet Neddy. They lived just off the Donegal coast on the little island of Owey, where my mother comes from. My grandfather died in 1963, so I don't remember him. But I was very close to my grandmother because she lived with us when I was growing up.

When my parents met for the first time, it certainly wasn't in the most romantic circumstances. Their first encounter was at the guttin'. And that's not a dance. They were both working at the dreadful task of cleaning out the entrails of fish at Lerwick in the Shetland Islands off Scotland. In those days it wasn't easy to eke out a living and you took whatever work was going. It was an awful life, but they made the most of it and they had good times too, judging by the stories that were told. Love blossomed between my parents and they married a year later, in 1948. I've always found it strange the way fate works. Burtonport to Owey Island is only four miles to the shore and then fifteen minutes on a currach. And they went all the way to the Shetland Islands before they met!

They had five children: John, Margaret (Margo), Kathleen, James and yours truly. And I was born on 12 December, 1961, in the local Dungloe Hospital. Wasn't that a great day for the world!! My brother John, the eldest in the family, is thirteen years older than me. He's married with two children, lives in Burtonport and works in a fish-processing plant in Killybegs. Kathleen is a housewife, mother-of-four and she lives at home in Kincasslagh. Margaret, who is better known as Margo, became a household name in Ireland as a singer, long before anyone had heard of me. She's just over ten years older than me and, like myself, she loves the stage and is still going as strong as ever. James, who is just four years older than me, works in a Dublin bar and I think everyone knows him because he's such a character. He's also married and has three children. He's well-known in GAA circles, especially the Gaelic football scene, and has a great knowledge of the sport.

In Ireland, I've frequently been called a 'Mammy's boy'. It's usually mentioned in derogatory terms. But, I suppose I am a Mammy's boy, because my father died when I was only six years old. And, being the youngest of the Bosco bunch, I was with her the longest and I'm probably the closest to her. I remember very little about my father. Apart from the fact that he died when I was so young, he worked away from home for six months out of every year. My father was a migrant labourer and, like a lot of other men in the area, the only work available in those days was in Scotland where he secured employment tattie hokin' [picking potatoes] and doing general work on farms. When I think about it now, it must have been a heart-breaking experience for my parents, having to suffer an enforced separation like that. It was a tough life for my father, living in poor accommodation in Scotland and trying to scrape enough money together to support a young family. And it eventually took its toll on his health. He was only forty-nine years old when he died from a massive heart attack in August 1968.

I'm not sure what awareness I had of his death, because I remember playing cowboys and Indians during the period of the wake. But I must have been very upset at the funeral, probably because everyone else was upset, as I remember a neighbour, Jim Nancy, taking me away and giving me icecream in his house. My mother was very distressed because they had been very happy. And at the time he was living at home after giving up the working stints in Scotland. Life has cruel twists and turns.

I only really know my father through other people. They say he was a very good man, with a quiet personality. He was fairly tall and at the time of his death he was very over-weight.

The only vague memory I have of my father is accompany-ing him down to the 'Port [Burtonport] in Jim Nancy's bread-van when he was returning to Scotland on one occasion. I remember him going off and I came back home with Jim. I do recall being very annoyed with him when he'd return from Scotland. I used to sleep with my mother when he was away and, of course, I'd be evicted from the bed when he came home. My reaction used to be, 'Why can't he sleep somewhere else?'

I don't know if my father's death had a psychological effect on me. I sometimes wonder would I be a stronger individual if he had been around when I was growing up. I never had a male role model, a man around me to look up to. But it wasn't until I was in my teens and the other fellas were doing things with their fathers, that I felt a sense of loss. And I also felt a sense of resentment. I don't think my father's death affected me. Not strongly. But the lack of a man around me did something to me, I believe. Maybe that's why I'm gentle in my ways. I wonder if he'd been there would he have made me stronger. But I would have hated my mother to have got married again.

My mother has been the big influence in my life. I love her dearly and I have tremendous admiration for the way she reared the family after our father died. It must have been a great struggle for her because my father never earned enough money to put by savings for a rainy day. So, I don't think she had anything at all when he died. Whatever the widow's pension was – and it wasn't a lot – she paid the bills out of it. And she used to knit sweaters and send them to America. She was very self-sufficient, really a strong character, and she was very good to us. Being the youngest, I was probably spoilt in a way. But I wasn't over-spoilt. I never grew up expecting much and I think that's all due to my mother. I never wanted for anything, but I was also cute enough not to look for things that I knew I couldn't get. I knew what the limitations were. Even to this day, I'm not motivated by money. The money is a by-product of what I've always wanted to do.

My ambition now for my mother is that she would be as comfortable and secure as she made us feel. I never felt insecure with her. And anywhere she went, I went too. She was strict with us, I suppose, to a certain extent. She was always adamant that we wouldn't drink or smoke. I never wanted to, but I think the fact that she was so dead against it, kept me away from it too. Her advice to us was always sound. She kept a watchful eye on her brood, making sure that we never got into trouble. I remember being late coming home from the youth club one night – and I was walking up the road with two pals when I saw her coming looking for me! She was giving out and I was really embarrassed. I think she took it hard and still finds it hard to realise that I grew up. But she's good at it now. And I think that where she helped me to grow up, I'm helping her to realise that I have grown up.

I still like to think that I have respect for her and that I think a great deal of her and that I'm very appreciative of all that she did for us as a family. I suppose that's why it doesn't bother me when people say, 'he's a Mammy's boy.' It's probably a tribute to the relationship that I have with her. But I think people over-do it too. I'm not still hanging onto my mother's apronstrings. I do my own thing. She's not still pulling the strings.

MY WONDERLAND

Although I was never conscious of it as a wee lad, I did grow up in poor circumstances. But I obviously had a happy childhood, because looking back I have fond memories of that era. The house which was our home during my early years was very basic. It was an old-fashioned two-storey residence with an open hearth fire that had pots hanging from crooks and simmering over hot coals. Even the scones (as we called the bread and cakes) were baked in a pot 'oven' on the open fire. My grandmother used to say that she carried stones for the building of the house, which was erected in the late 1800s. We didn't own it. It belonged to my mother's cousin, and it is still there today, situated across from the council house which later became our home.

Our living conditions were fairly primitive. There was no water supply laid on and we had to draw water from our neighbour Annie's well across the road; we didn't have a bathroom and the toilet was a tin hut across the road. When I think of it now, that was quite incredible, considering it was only twenty-five years ago. I can recall only one family who had a flush toilet and I used to be mesmerised by it.

Nowadays, children are bathed on a regular basis, sometimes daily. But in those days there was a big 'scrub up' in a tub in front of the open fire in the kitchen-cum-livingroom on a Saturday night. And that was it. I don't remember getting washed during the week. It wasn't that I was a dirty wee bugger or anything, but I don't remember being washed every night. There wasn't so much emphasis on that in those days. We must have been rotten at school during the week! I often think now, how did the teachers put up with us then?

In 1967, a year before my father died, we got a new house from Donegal County Council. At the time, it was like moving into a space ship. It had a bathroom. And a toilet. And taps. God, the fun I had turning on and off those taps, watching the water gushing out of the little pipes. Magic. Boy, we were really coming up in the world! It was wonderful moving into that grand house.

The world beyond in those days wasn't very important. To me, nothing existed outside our little close-knit community. Kincasslagh, a small fishing village on the north-west coast of Ireland where I grew up, was like a wonderland. It was really remote and rugged. But when I reflect on that period of my life, it's not so much the village and surrounding area that stirs my imagination. It's the memory of the people.

When I think back now, a sea of faces comes to my mind. There was Nora Dan, the most wonderful human being you could ever hope to meet. When people talk about Nora Dan, it's with so much affection. Nora lived up at the graveyard, about two miles from me. She was a bit eccentric, but she loved people, and callers to her home were welcomed with open arms. The house couldn't be full enough for her. And, indeed, it wasn't only humans you'd find there. You'd often see the hens putting their heads through the door, and Nora's reaction would be, 'Shush! Who invited you for tea?'

I remember one day, Nora got involved in a discussion with my sister Kathleen about my future. There was great concern about what was going to become of me when I left school, because it was well known that I was absolutely useless with my hands. I might as well not have been born with hands – they were only there to finish off my arms. People in those days judged you by how you performed at manual tasks, working in the fields or in the bog cutting turf [sections of peat used as natural fuel]. As far as that kind of work was concerned, I was the village idiot. I couldn't master the simplest manual skill. So the big worry was, 'How's poor Daniel going to survive in the world at all, at all?'

'Well now, I don't know what you're going to do,' said Nora.

My sister Kathleen suggested: 'Maybe he'll go to the bank?'

'No,' said Nora, 'you wouldn't have laces in your shoes till you were a bank manager. And there are so few managers. You'd have to be a clerk and you'd have nothing. Well, now, maybe the Guards [police]?'

But Kathleen pointed out: 'Sure he has bad eyesight.'

'Oh,' said Nora, 'you need the sight. If you were over at the turn [bend on the road] and there was after being a robbery in the village, you'd need to be able to read the number of their car.'

Poor Nora, she was perplexed. She sauntered off, shaking her head. What was going to become of young Daniel?

Then there was John Phil, a huge, rotund, jolly man, much loved by everyone in the village. He was incredible, the unusual things he did. I really believe that if the Leaning Tower of Pisa hadn't been built, he would have got around to doing it. For instance, he was a big, big man and he bought a mini car. How he ever got into it is beyond me. He used to travel everywhere in second gear and you'd hear him coming miles away. John was very self-sufficient. He liked to fish and I recall how he used to make flies out of the feathers from hens. There was no such thing as a Black-and-Decker drill in those days and whenever he needed to bore a hole, he put a poker in the fire and when it was red hot he'd run out the door with it to the area where he was working! There was Pat Neil Pat, who had a big house in the village and he seemed to be involved in everything. He was the harbour master and he had houses for rent. I remember he had a big car, which was really rare in those days. And he always drove at his own pace, maybe ten or fifteen miles an hour, no matter where he'd be going. I recall one occasion when the politician Neil Blaney was canvassing in County Donegal, Pat took Annie McGarvey and myself with him in the car to hear Blaney's oration. We followed the politician's cavalcade around the county, but by the time we arrived in each town, Blaney was finishing his speech! We never did get to hear that speech, but there was no way that Pat would drive any faster.

Josie McGarvey was the village blacksmith and he lived next-door to us with his daughter, Annie (as I mentioned, we drew water from their well). She had a cow, a donkey called Johnny and hens. She was like family to me. When I was a young schoolboy, if Annie was sick I'd put Johnny in the shed in the evening; I'd take in the eggs and the turf for the fire and I'd do her messages [shopping]. Annie used to have a pit of tatties [potatoes] out in the field and in the wintertime she'd cover them with hay to protect them from the frost. She was also the only one living near us who had hay, and the making of hay down in the field was a big day. It wouldn't be a day's work now with the new machinery, but it was then.

Those were the kind of people who figured in my childhood. They weren't hip. They weren't trendy types. They were plain, ordinary, unpretentious folk who lived at a much slower pace than we do today. It was a tough life, but there was a great spirit of neighbourliness, with people helping other people whenever the need arose. They had their own fund of stories. They created their own fun. And so many of them were such colourful characters.

Because emigration was very much an enforced facet of Irish

life in those days, as it is today, there were very few teenagers or young adults in the village. Once people reached a certain age, they all left home in search of work abroad. So, the people in my childhood were all very old.

Because we were the only house in the village where an island woman lived – as I said, my Mother came from Owey – the islanders from Owey used to stay overnight with us whenever they came to the mainland. The men from Tory Island used to stay too. Eamon and Anton were two old men who called regularly and they'd sleep in a sitting position on chairs by the open fire. There was no limit to the amount of people who would come to stay in our home. They'd roast fish – mackerel and herring – over the fire and there were always great sing-songs.

Like most youngsters from the country, I had a number of pets to play with as a child. We had cats and a series of dogs, of course, but I also had a rabbit and a pigeon called Jacko. He was a wild pigeon and I clipped his wings so he couldn't fly. Wasn't that an awful thing to do? The rabbit was a wee white one and he was lovely. The whole lot of them used to sleep around the fire, including the pigeon. As he couldn't fly, he had nowhere else to go! So the dog and the cats and the pigeon and the rabbit all slept together in harmony, they were so used to one another. I loved pets at that time, but now I've become allergic to all things like that.

We had a dog called Rover who used to go away on the ram-dam [the hunt] after lady dogs. He'd be away for a couple of days, then he'd return. That was always a wild day as he'd get battered by my mother who had been worried and was hoping she'd teach him to stay at home. He'd know he was in for it too, because he'd be crying coming up the hill to our house. He'd come in looking sheepish, his head hanging low, knowing full well what was in store for him.

Mother would be out, calling: 'Where were you?'

And our John would say: 'Tell her, Rover. Tell her.'

One time he was away for so long that when he came back he was as thin as a whistle. But he got a great *fáilte* [welcome] that day. He didn't know what was happening, because he was expecting the usual trouncing! He was a mongrel, part sheepdog, and we all adored him, despite his wayward habits.

I was with my mother most of the time, but whenever she wanted to slip away without me, she used to say, 'You can't come with me, Daniel. I'm going to confession.' I always accepted that excuse and never kicked up a fuss. But, subconsciously, I must have realised that she was trying to pull a fast one on me, because one day I was going up the road and Rover was tagging along. I didn't want him with me, so I turned back to my mother and shouted, 'Mammy, tell Rover I'm going to confession!' It's funny how a child's mind works.

Eventually, Rover died from old age. The very same day – God, you'd think he knew – our James was bringing home a wee white terrier. But didn't Rover die half-an-hour before the terrier arrived. That's the truth. There was a wild bit of crying altogether when poor Rover died. We, of course, called the terrier Rover then. He used to need a haircut every so often, because he was always messing around in ditches and picking up dirt. My mother used to give him some kind of tablets, I don't know what they were, to sedate him while the grooming operation was being performed. But this night, anyway, she went through the same procedure and sure poor Rover never woke up. He had died from an overdose. He must have been only about three months old. I was very upset and ordered everyone to clear off! That death finished it – there were no more dogs in our house after that.

We had some lovely cats, but there was one big red tomcat and he'd nearly eat you. We couldn't catch him. He was completely wild. My mother did everything to try and kill him. He even got his foot run over by some sort of machinery and he ended up with only half a leg, but he still survived. He was horrible.

One day, a neighbour, Mary Hugo, was crying about all her cats.

'And what happened?' my mother asked.

'I'll tell you what happened now,' sobbed poor Mary. 'There was whiskey poured into the milk in the cats' dish and the cats all died.'

Well, my mother couldn't wait to get home to get the whiskey bottle out. But do you think it killed him? Not at all. He only thrived. Mind you, he disappeared shortly after that. He either got the message, or he met a fate that I was never told about.

My playground as a child also included Owey Island. I spent my holidays there as a youngster, running wild. One abiding memory is that the sun always shone on the island in the mornings. There was no rain that I can remember. Fishing was the main thing carried on there and I can recall the men going out in the early hours of the morning – you'd hear the sound of wellington boots on the gravel. A wellington boot makes a different noise to a shoe, and I can still hear that sound – the wellington army off to the fishing. I never went with them. I didn't like the sea. I was always kind of afraid of it. But I loved that island. There was a wonderful silence on it. It was another world.

It's an uninhabited island today, but way back then, my granduncle Andy lived there with his wife Ellen and son Neilie. Andy was the postman. Then Neilie became the postman when he retired. I also used to stay with my Uncle James and his wife, Peggy.

There were only two families on the island that we weren't related to, so we were all *muintir* [the one people]. I'd spend my days swimming and playing with the other kids, especially Mary McGonagle, my cousin, who was two years older than me, and John Martin, who was a bit younger.

I remember, too, the dances in the school on Owey. It was like 'Little House on the Prairie'. If there was a party it was held in the school. One such function I recall there was for my mother's cousin Dominic McDevitt, when he returned home from America for a short holiday. Whenever an emigrant came home from the USA, everyone on the island turned out to meet the boat. At the time, there were up to a hundred people living on Owey – each family had ten or twelve children. And when someone was leaving the island for the States, every man, woman and child went down to the boat to see them off. I remember the great sadness that fell over the community when people were going away. The pain of emigration.

On the mainland where I lived, one of the biggest outings was to the bog for the cutting of the turf, which we used for fuel. I hated the bloody auld bog, but it was a grand day really. You'd get a lift up to the bog on the tractor, which was a big thrill way back then. And there'd be great feeds. Very often, there'd be lemonade which was a novelty at the time. I remember one house where the kids had Lucozade, Cidona and lemonade all the time and I thought they were really posh.

We didn't travel far from home in those days, but one time when we were small, my cousin James and his new bride Doreen came over on holidays. At the time, *The Sound Of Music* was on in the cinema in Donegal town, or so we thought. James and Doreen decided to go up to Donegal to see it and they took us along. It was like going to America, even though it was only slightly over forty miles. We set off in the car, James and Doreen, Mammy, Kathleen, my brother James and myself. We weren't far on the road when James got sick and vomited all over Mammy's new coat! Well, she clattered him at the side of the road. When we got there, *The Sound Of Music* wasn't on at all. Then our James demanded chips, and he after getting sick on the way up!

Before my father died, we often went to Derry on holidays during the summer. We stayed with a family friend called Leslie Harkin, down in Westland Street. That was a great treat for us kids. Even though I was very young, I can still remember that period so vividly. I particularly recall the type of things that only kids remember. Like the big park up beside the cathedral with its wonderful swings. That park was like Disneyland to us because we had no such attractions at home. The fun we had on those swings! We could happily have spent our young lives there. And I remember the man who used to come around in a van selling lemonade. He was like the Pied Piper, surrounded by kids clamouring for his goodies. What's seldom is wonderful.

My grandmother, Margaret Neddy from Owey Island, lived with us up to the time she died in 1973. I remember I used to sleep with her when we moved to our new home. She was a grand old lady, a real old-style woman. She had white hair tied in a bun, wee glasses, long skirts and a shawl. She always dressed in black. Granny regularly visited the island. Even on her ninetieth birthday she put on her wellington boots and was brought over on the small boat. On that same occasion a friend, Biddy Tague, came over to visit us and I recall Granny showing Biddy what she was wearing. It was her wedding dress. It was a dark colour and she still had it. Imagine that!

GROWING UP

My teddy bear accompanied me on my first day at school. He was bigger than me, so he gave me moral support and I didn't get upset or lonely for home. Our school, Belcruit national school was just a two-room building. It was built in 1964, so it was fairly new when I started there in 1967. It was a mile-and-a-half from home, which was a long walk for a wee child. In later years during the autumn months, the return journey often took me three hours because I'd stop to pick blackberries growing wild in the ditches along the meandering path. My teacher almost all the way through school was Miss Gallagher, who later became Mrs. Logue, and I don't think I ever gave her much trouble. I was always reasonably well-behaved. But I suppose I got the odd scutch [slap] when I deserved it.

Miss Gallagher was a good teacher and I think I was fairly bright. I wasn't a genius, but I wasn't stupid either. Our James would have been cleverer than me. But I got on all right and I enjoyed the days there. I loved maths – I always wanted to be ahead of the rest of the class. It was my best subject, so I always wanted to be doing maths. In particular, I loved algebra. Later on, I had notions of becoming an accountant, but they never came to anything.

I suppose the highlights of those early schooldays in Ireland are centred around the Roman Catholic religious ceremonies of First Communion and Confirmation. My First Communion in 1969 was a sad event because my father had died the previous year. I remember that having a bearing on it. The suit I wore had been worn by my brother John when he'd made his First Communion thirteen years previously. Nowadays, when children make their First Communion it's a big family occasion, with meals out in restaurants and so forth. But I got icecream in the village on the walk home from church and that was my special treat.

Confirmation is another special day in the life of a young Catholic boy. There was a big lead-up to it, as you had to learn the catechism in detail. Mrs. Logue was obviously a very good teacher because I remember that on Confirmation day I actually thought something was going to physically happen to me, that I was going to experience something special. I watched my friends going up to the bishop and as they returned I was thinking: 'Oh God, he's got IT. She's got IT.' Then I went up myself and I got nothing, as I thought. But now, when I look back, I realise the importance of it as far as my religion is concerned. The suit I wore on my Confirmation day was bought for me by my sister Margaret [Margo] and it was too big. In those days, there were no professional photographic sessions to capture the special occasion. Our neighbour, Annie McGarvey, took the photographs at my First Communion and Confirmation. She was our Lichfield. Whatever was to be recorded, she recorded it. Annie has photographs dating back to 1937, the year she first got her camera.

The summers in those days seemed to be endless. Looking back, they were such carefree days. We were so innocent. Life was simple – just wonderful, fun-filled days playing silly games like cowboys and Indians, with sticks for guns and bows and arrows. There were no high-tech toys at that time. I loved the sun and I've always been an easy-going guy – it takes a lot to freak me out over something. I'm probably like that by nature, but I also believe that one of the people who helped to condition me into that mood was a lady called Mrs. Ashforth, who was a native of County Mayo, but lived in our area. My cousin, Mary McGonagle, and myself used to spend a lot of time up at Mrs. Ashforth's house when we were teenagers. We did odd jobs for her, like cutting the grass. Mrs. Ashforth had a great outlook on life. She loved the sun, just like myself, and in the summertime she would bask in it all day long. Whenever she'd see people rushing around in the good weather, she'd always remark: 'There's one thing that will never go away and that's the dust. It will always wait on us.' She was implying that everything else will wait too. I remember thinking, 'How right she is.' She's a wonderful lady and I still keep in contact with her by letter.

Christmas was a great time too. We lived on The Smith's Brae, so-called because Josie McGarvey, the blacksmith, lived at the top of it. ('Brae' is the Scottish for hill, and there's a big Scottish influence in our locality because so many people worked in Scotland.) When it snowed we had such fun on our sleighs. We'd go right down the hill into the village and if you were really good you'd make a turn and continue on down to the strand. At night time, we used to throw water on the brae to make sure it would be really slippy for the sleighs the following morning.

People at that time had a very casual attitude to injuries. A gash that nowadays would lead to all hell breaking loose in the family home and a frantic trip to the doctor's surgery with the injured child, hardly raised an eyebrow during my childhood days. I suppose people had a fear of the doctor's surgery. Or perhaps they were just a tougher species then. They had probably become immune to cuts and bruises which were a regular feature of daily life, with so many people engaged in manual jobs. A personal injury that has remained in my memory is the day I fell on the road and slashed my face. Sure,

I thought I was killed! There was blood pumping out of my face and I thought the skin was hanging off. I couldn't understand why my mother was remaining so calm and me about to die, as I thought. There was no ambulance called. Or no doctor. The only 'surgery' performed was done by my mother when she rubbed butter into the wound. Butter had some great uses in those days. In this case, it was applied to remove the tar from the cut. I still have a facial scar from that incident. But you would hardly notice it now because the crow's feet, or laughter lines if you prefer! have joined up with it.

One Christmas, my friend Anne Sharkey, along with her sister and two other girls, decided that we would do the 'Mummers'. That's a local tradition in which people dress up in costume and go singing in the local houses and bars. Instead of singing, however, we decided to do a full Nativity play. And we made a lot of money – about £50 each, which was a fortune to us at that time. So every year after that, even when we were at secondary school [second level], we did the 'Mummers'. We'd do four or five nights and call to all the pubs. The customers were full of the joys of life with the booze and they were extra generous to us as a result.

Of all the toys I ever got for Christmas, the one I remember most was a big, red plastic bus, which had no moving parts. But I used to sit on it and pretend I was driving it and I loved that red bus. I always sang in the choir at midnight Mass on Christmas Eve and that's something I still do to this day. Nowadays, I'm not a great Christmas person. I love the ceremony that is midnight Mass, but I don't share the feeling that some people have for Christmas. It's not that I dislike it, but I don't build myself up for it like most people do. I love going to midnight Mass in Kincasslagh because it's the only time in the whole year when everyone seems to be together under the same roof. You look around and there's a sea of faces that you know. The emigrants are home from abroad and everyone is acknowledging each other with nods. It's a very special occasion. Our chapel is close to the shore and when you go down to Mass on Christmas Eve, it's a beautiful scene, particularly if the moon is out and the tide is in.

From about the age of nine, I worked in The Cope, a general store in the village. And I feel that The Cope and the people it introduced me to, had a huge influence in shaping the person that I am today. It was my first introduction to dealing with people whom I had never met before. I was always very reserved – and still am in certain ways today – but working in The Cope gave me the ability to reach out, and it helped me to converse well with strangers. The Cope was a store that had everything from animal feed to wellington boots and general household items and food. I started off sweeping the floor and weighing the corn, layers' mash, chick mash and corn cake for the cows. They also had a van on the road, a travelling store selling to people who lived in outlying areas and, eventually, I worked on that. For a lot of people who lived in that part of County Donegal, the Cope van would be their memory of me. That's how I became known to a lot of people around my area and its environs long before I made my name as a singer.

It was a good time for me. I loved going out on the van. People would invite you into their home for tea. Betty Doogan's, I recall, was one place where we always got something to eat – the fish fingers, in particular, I remember so well. On other days when I did relief work in another Cope in nearby Annagry, I'd get my dinner in Biddy The Butcher's and the dessert would always be arctic roll, which was sponge cake with icecream in the middle. Delicious.

While working on the van, I met Protestants for the first time.

I grew up at a time when there was no real contact between Protestants and Catholics. There was a lot of ignorance about each other's way of life. For instance, I had this impression that Protestants wouldn't like country music because I liked it. And the first time I went into a Protestant church, I thought that all hell would break loose – I was afraid to stand up in case I'd be struck dead or deformed! And I thought I'd be condemned to hell for going in. But the Protestants I met on the van, the Boyds, opened my eyes to the fact that they were just the same as me.

I continued working in The Cope every summer, until I was fourteen. I also worked there for two hours every evening after school and all day Saturday. My wages at the end of the week were £2 and I saved the money for my annual holiday to Scotland. I travelled over on my own by boat – wasn't I a very brave young lad? – and I stayed with relatives in Glasgow, Edinburgh, Perth and Callendar. When I perform in Edinburgh nowadays, I often remember the cuckoo clock in Prince's Street Gardens. I used to be mesmerised by the cuckoo coming out of the clock on the hour. A crowd always gathered to watch it and it took me a long time to discover that it was a mechanical cuckoo. I always thought he was real!

I liked shopping in Edinburgh and was always on the lookout for a bargain. On one occasion, I bought two pairs of shoes with gold tips on the toes. I thought I was a real dandy and couldn't wait to show them off in the village when I got back. Sunday Mass provided me with a great opportunity, so off I strutted on my first weekend home. I was proudly putting each foot forward, hoping that people would notice.

Coming out of the church, a fella said to me, 'You have a fine pair of shoes on.'

'Do you like them?' I asked, as proud as punch.

'You got a quare bargain at £4.99,' he smirked.

The sale sticker was still on the sole of the shoe and everyone had seen it when I knelt down at the altar for Communion. God, that was embarrassing.

I stayed in national school till I was in seventh class. I was man big. Then I went up to Dungloe for second level. Dungloe secondary school was amalgamated with the technical school in Loughanure and you had to attend the Tech, as it was known, for the first year. The secondary school was more academic, whereas the Tech covered practical subjects like woodwork. By the time the year was up, I had become friendly with P.J. Sweeney and Patrick Kyles. They were very good with their hands and excellent at the practical subjects. Because they were staying on in the Tech part of the school, 'muggins' decided to stay on too, even though I was useless with my hands and hated woodwork. I was also useless at science and mechanical drawing. I was just hopeless at those subjects and I had no interest in them.

Poor Cundy, he was a retired headmaster who was teaching woodwork. I remember one day I made a dove-tail joint and I thought it was fairly good. All the good joints used to be put on display. And I thought this was a real humdinger. So, Cundy inspected the joint anyway, and handed it back to me.

I said to him, thinking it was heading for the mantelpiece, 'What'll I do with it now, Sir?'

And he came over really close to me and said, 'Throw it in the fire.'

But the Tech in Loughanure was great all the same. Cassie's shop was nearby and we all trooped down there in the middle of the day. We used to buy sweets and eat them sitting around the fire. Anne Sharkey was my best friend at school. And if Anne and her classmates were doing cookery during domestic science classes, I'd go in and join them. I had this way with me that I could get in through the eye of a needle. I shouldn't have been in there, but Miss Keady, their teacher, turned a blind eye. So, I'd be in with the girls, eating what they cooked.

Miss Breslin was our book-keeping teacher. She wore a headscarf and had her own inimitable style about her. She would sit at her desk peering down at us, chanting: 'Draw a red line, skip a blue line. Draw a red line, skip a blue line ...' It became her sort of catchphrase and even to this day, whenever people from her class meet, they go: 'Draw a red line, skip a blue line ...' P.J., Patrick and myself were good at the book-keeping and we were the only boys in the class. Miss Breslin used to say to the girls, 'It's a wonder ye wouldn't be like these three fellas up here!' We were her pride and joy.

Although we didn't know it at the time, she used to smoke. Her book-keeping class was a double class, so she'd leave the room for a quick puff in the middle of it. One day she went out and left her scarf behind her. I went up to her desk, put on her scarf and began mimicking her: 'Draw a red line, skip a blue line ...' Well, didn't she come back and catch me at it! She walked up to the desk and stood there stoney-faced while I took off the scarf and went back to my desk. She sat down and never said a word. But she didn't have to. The shame of being caught making fun of a woman who thought I was a saint was enough punishment.

In the wintertime, when I was in secondary school, I used to hate getting up on the cold mornings to head off on the early bus. I'd stick my head out from under the blankets and see the steam from my breath almost freezing before my eyes in the bedroom. A glance at the window would reveal that 'Jack Frost' had arrived. There was no central heating in the houses in those days and no electric blankets. At that time, only my mother and I were in the house. I always got up, prepared my own breakfast and got myself out to school. But occasionally I just wouldn't have the motivation to go in and I'd say to my mother, who'd still be in bed, 'There's snow today!' And she'd say, 'Oh, if it's a bad day, maybe you shouldn't bother going.' Well, I'd be back under those warm blankets like lightning. By the time my mother got up there wouldn't even be a trace of frost on the ground, and she'd throw me a quizzical look. 'Ah sure, the snow thawed out,' I'd explain. Amazingly, I always got away with that stunt.

The second-level school was a good time for me. I got on well with all the teachers. In our fourth year, we went to France. That was a wonderful experience. It was in 1979 and that was a fair step thirteen years ago – from Donegal to France. We went on the boat from Rosslare to Le Havre. I remember we were singing all the time on the Metro in Paris. It was the year Cathal Dunne represented Ireland in the Eurovision Song Contest with 'Happy Man'. And we were all singing 'Happy Man'.

During my schooldays, I got many opportunities to show off my singing talents in the local community. I loved being in the limelight and I never needed any encouragement to sing for an audience. One vehicle which introduced me to the stage in those days was the local variety concert which was staged in the parish hall. Those concerts, scripted and performed by people in the community, provided hours of live entertainment. And they unearthed the many hidden talents of neighbours, who impressed all and sundry with their acting, singing and musical skills. The variety concert was a great tradition, with people staging their home-produced shows in small towns and villages throughout the land before the advent of television. They united young and old and gave people, particularly teenagers, the confidence that comes from performing in public. Lots of people around the country met their partners through such productions, because they brought together people whose lives might not have crossed otherwise. They were a real asset to the community. When I was a youngster, there were always dances in the village hall on a Sunday afternoon. Rose Marie Brennan, an aunt of the Irish group Clannad and of Enya, was the resident entertainer. She sang and played the accordion. The adults danced the soles off their shoes while the children caused havoc chasing each other around the dancefloor.

When I was in my 'teens the big sporting event every Sunday was the regatta. The skiff races were really exciting and involved the entire community. I wasn't part of the team, but I was a great supporter. Our team was one of the best, so they won a lot of big events. The support they received at competitions around the country was fantastic – two hundred people often travelled with them to cheer them on.

The *céilí* [traditional dancing] was another great form of entertainment in our area. It were much more enjoyable than an ordinary dance because you could get up and dance with anyone in a 'set' without asking. There was also a great tradition of having tea at the *céilí*, which gave people the opportunity to sit and chat together. I still like to attend a *céilí* when I go home to Kincasslagh.

At school, although I had friends, I was a bit of a loner. I never really liked playing football. And I was the kind of individual who wouldn't do something I didn't like, just because everyone else was doing it. As a result, I used to get a lot of slagging. People ask me now, 'How do you put up with all the slating you're subjected to?' Sure I grew up with it – and I still dislike some of my fellow-students as a result of it. I was soft and they gave me such a hard time. They called me a sissy because I'd get up to let some old person have a seat on the bus. They laughed at me for that kind of thing. If you weren't involved in causing trouble, you'd be called a sissy. Maybe it was also due to the fact that I spent more time with Anne Sharkey than I did with fellas. I suppose that's something that's difficult to understand. But as I grew older I realised that it can happen with a lot of people, that their friend can be a girl – and just be a friend. I think everyone thought that Anne and I would eventually get married. Even to this day, I could travel from here to eternity with Anne and really enjoy it.

Anne was a year ahead of me at school, so we weren't in the same class. But whenever I had a free class, I'd slip into Anne's classroom to join her and her friends and we'd have a great laugh. I was good *craic* [fun], there's no doubt about it, and I'd have all the gossip. God, I wouldn't gossip now. Isn't that funny? I suppose as I grew older I developed a different perspective. But, looking back, it wasn't malicious gossip or anything like that, it was just harmless fun.

So, because I hung out with the girls I came in for a really hard time from some of the lads in the school. And I would never stand up for myself. I'd run a mile rather than fight. I hated swearing and I never used swear words. Nowadays, I let out an odd *focal mór* as we called the swear words, but I never cursed in those days. So I was seen then, as now, as being 'Mr. Perfect'. I grew up with the jibes, but that doesn't mean I want them to continue. But I suppose they will.

I didn't do well in my Leaving Certificate [Irish equivalent of the O and A Levels]. I didn't really work at school in my last year or so. I worked for the teachers whom I thought were good. I thought I was working for them when, in fact, I should have been working for myself. I think all children are like that. It's not till you get older that you realise you should have been putting in the effort for yourself. I always hated exams and I never performed well at them. They made me nervous and I could never concentrate. My best subject was accountancy – but I'll never forget that exam. I just freaked out. I still feel that there should be some different form of assessment, on your performance over a number of years rather than what you produce in exams over a few hours. I did honours [higher level] in English, Irish, accountancy and economics. I only got the honour in economics, but I passed everything. But it was a good enough Leaving Cert. to get me into Galway Regional College.

Margo

My sister Margaret – better known in Ireland as the singer, Margo – has had a big influence on my career. Margaret, who is just over ten years older than me, started singing in a band when she was only twelve years old! As a teenager, she'd travel home through the night in the back of a van from a dance and snatch a couple of hours' sleep in the early morning before heading off to school. It was the true showbiz tradition of hard graft that got her to the top of her chosen career. Growing up, I don't think I was conscious of the volume of her success. But I was aware that she was different to other kids' sisters. The first time I remember taking notice of her as a singer was in 1969, when I was only eight. She had a hit record with a song called, 'Dear God', and it was played on the radio. I thought she was great. As I grew older, I used to get away at weekends because my mother would travel to see her perform and she took me with her. It was on those occasions that I got my first taste of the stage, because Margaret used to get me up to sing with her – I would have been nine, ten or eleven.

Margo became a household name and a really big star throughout Ireland. Everyone in our area was very proud of her and they all shared her success. The first time she had a No. 1 record with a song called, 'I'll Forgive And I'll Try To Forget', there were wild celebrations in the locality. That was in the early seventies and I remember a cavalcade of cars turned out to meet her and there was a big party in the village hall. We had a great night, singing and dancing. Another landmark in her career was the night she appeared on the 'Late Late Show' for the first time. The Irish TV show, hosted by Gay Byrne, is an institution. At the time, it was broadcast every Saturday night and I swear the streets and country roads were deserted while it was on. Certainly, anyone who had a television at that time was glued to the 'Late Late Show' on a Saturday night. It was compulsive viewing. And appearing on the show with Gay Byrne was like appearing with God. The night Margaret made her debut on the phenomenally successful show was also cause for great celebration in our home upon her return from Dublin. All the neighbours came in and there was a big hooley. I remember her performance on the 'Late Late' that night. She sang a song called 'The Bonny Irish Boy'. My father gave her that song before he died – he wrote it down and taught her the air. Margaret recorded it, but the day it was due out, our father died. He never heard that record.

Around that time, a guy called Hughie Green had a talent show on British TV called 'Opportunity Knocks'. My grand-mother used to watch it and she was convinced that Hughie Green was waving at her. So convinced, in fact, that she used to wave back at him! The night Margaret appeared on the 'Late Late Show', she told Granny to put on her best outfit. On her return from Dublin, Margaret was told what Granny had been wearing that night in front of the telly. When Margaret later described the outfit to her, Granny was astounded. 'Well, good God, that Hughie Green can see me after all,' she gasped.

I became more aware of Margaret's success as I grew older. And I was quite happy to be Margo's brother. It was a great perk. Margaret shared the rewards of her success with the family. She was very good to us. After Granny died, she sent Mammy and myself to America on a holiday. The year was 1973 and for me it was like going to the moon. I was only twelve years old. Boy, did I have a good time out there! Although we were there only for a few weeks, I came back

I was only a year old when this photo was taken and someone obviously thought I'd look better wearing 'specs'.

Here I am as a baby with big brother James.

Above: My grandparents on my mother's side: James and Margaret McGonagle, pictured in 1959.

Left: My First Communion in 1968. I was seven.

Above: My father and mother pictured in 1948, the year of their wedding.
Below: Another special occasion, my Confirmation, in1972, aged 11.

Above: Posing for the camera – an official photo session, in 1990.
Below: From the family album in 1980 when I became godfather
to my sister Kathleen's new arrival, Patricia. The little boy is my
nephew John Francis.

Above: Here I am performing with Elvis Presley's backing group The Jordanaires at Fanfare, the American showcase for country artistes in Nashville. Right: Performing on the famous Ralph Emery show in Nashville [1988].

Above: Capturing the atmosphere in Nashville. Below: Thumbs up for the 'The Last Waltz', with top Nashville Producer Allen Reynolds, who has also worked with Garth Brooks, Emmylou Harris, Don Williams and Crystal Gayle.

...e made it to New York's famous Carnegie Hall. It's a long way from Kincasslagh, County Donegal. That 1991 concert is one I'll always remember.

Above: I don't always get the opportunity to watch the British TV soap, EastEnders, but I did get to meet some of the cast in 1988. They include Michael Cashman, Letitia Dean, Gillian Tayleforth and Susan Tully.

Left: Standing by her man...Your's truly with Tammy Wynette, pictured at Wembley, London in 1988.

What a thrill! One of the advantages of being a successful singer is that you get to meet some of the most beautiful women in the world. Here I am with country legend Dolly Parton and British TV and radio personality Gloria Hunniford.

Above: My TV special 'Country Comes Home', recorded in Dublin in 1989, gave me the opportun
to team up with some of the country scene's most talented performers, including Charley Pride a
The Judds. Below: Interview time, with BBC Radio 2 country music presenter Wally Whyton.

*My wildest dream comes true. Performing with my idol, American country music legend
Loretta Lynn on my Irish TV series, 'The Daniel O'Donnell Show', see my story
on the 'Coalminer's Daughter' in chapter 8.*

Top: Acknowledging the warmth and affection of the people at the end of another show [Fairfield Hall, Croydon, England]. Above: Touching hands at The Galtymore, Cricklewood, London, in 1990.

Above: The Mullaghduff Fife and Drum Band, of which I was a member as a wee fella, making a presentation to me at home when I was awarded the title Ireland's Entertainer Of The Year.

Right: The TV 'King', the singer and the priest. Here I am with 'Uncle Gaybo', host of one of the world's longest-running TV chat shows. Gay Byrne and his 'Late Late Show' are an institution in Ireland. We're pictured with Ireland's best known priest, Fr Brian D'Arcy, showbiz chaplain, a country music fan, journalist and broadcaster.

*I've become a soccer fan since Donegal's Packie Bonner captured my imagination
with his outstanding performance as goalkeeper on the Republic of
Ireland team in the 1990 World Cup.*

The big event of the year in my area – the Mary From Dungloe festival.
I never miss it. See you there!

My, how the crowds flock to the 'Mary' festival.

Above: Maybe I should take up modelling? Here I am posing for another publicity photograph in 1991.

Left: Fans come in all shapes and sizes. But a dog? Tinker, from Glasgow, is an official member of my Fan Club.

with a 'Yankee' accent. We had relatives living in New Jersey, including my mother's sister, Maggie. The first night in Bayonne, there was a party thrown in our honour and we were treated like celebrities. I sang for them and loved all the attention. Everything in America was so vast, compared to home. The roads had lane after lane and there were cars and lights everywhere. That's something I wasn't used to. The buildings in New York went up into the sky. And when you went out you'd never see anybody you knew. That was strange for me, because I knew everybody at home.

There must have been no Pepsi-Cola at home at that time, because I remember Pepsi-Cola and me, we had a great affair when I was in America. And the icecream was just beautiful. That trip was a real dream. We came back with a mountain of gifts – a family of ten wouldn't have the amount of luggage we were carrying. Everything that was given to us, my mother took home. You couldn't see us behind the trolleys.

On the way back, we stopped in Killala, County Mayo, where Margaret was performing at a carnival dance and I got up to sing with her. I often went down to Killala on holidays to Martin Ford's pub. Martin used to take me out in the car and I'd sing in loads of pubs that we visited. We went to Belmullet one night to see Margaret perform in a venue called The Palm Court and I got up to sing with her that night, too. 'Little Cabin Home On The Hill' and 'The Philadelphia Lawyer' were my songs. That was all great experience for me. It was my intro-duction to the live music scene and I took to it like a fish to water. And that was Margaret's influence. Later, when I be-came established in my own right, Margaret and I recorded a duet together and it went to No.1 in the Irish hit parade. The song was called, 'Two's Company', and we are the only brother and sister ever to have a No.1 hit record in Ireland.

From the Graveyard to the Stage

Although I never had what people would term a 'proper' job after I left college, I was employed in some rather strange occupations during the summers leading up to my entry into the world of showbiz. I spent one summer working in a graveyard! I suppose you could call that a dead-end job! Well, you have to start somewhere. And sure wasn't Rod Stewart a grave-digger in his early days. So, I'm in good company. But I didn't have to dig graves, my task was to maintain the graveyard. I always hated that kind of work and spent most of my time sunbathing behind the headstones. I worked in Logue's store in the town of Dungloe for several weeks during another summer. I also secured employment on a local scheme, digging drains. I hated every minute of that. It was like working on a chain gang. That was in 1979 and the following year I progressed to washing dishes in Dublin's Central Hotel after completing my Leaving Certificate examination and leaving secondary school.

The summer of 1980 was a great period in my life. My brother James, who lives in Dublin, got me that job in the Central Hotel where he also worked. And it was there that I met Margaret Coyle and Maura Cullinane. We became great friends and were inseparable. I laughed my way through that whole summer. We had a ball, dancing every night in the Dublin clubs: The Ierne, The National, The Irish Club, The TV Club and The Olympic. These were dancing clubs which were mostly frequented by people from rural Ireland who were working in the capital. And they all featured the type of music that I enjoy. All the big names of the day were playing those venues at the time: Big Tom, Larry Cunningham, Philomena Begley, Patrice, Brian Coll and my own sister, Margo. The Irish Club was my favourite. There was a great buzz in it and I loved the formal-style dances, the waltzes, the quick-steps and the jives. I was never into disco dancing. Perhaps people might find it difficult to comprehend, but none of us got romantically involved. We went out together, we danced and had a laugh. And it never progressed beyond that.

I disliked the hotel work in the beginning because I was down in the lower kitchen, washing the pots and pans. But the situation improved when I was promoted to the upstairs kitchen, which involved washing the plates and cutlery. But the main advantage was that it was just off the diningroom and you felt you were closer to the action. I remember one night there was a mouse in the diningroom while customers were eating and I was sent out to discreetly catch it with a brush and pan. And me dead scared of mice! Because I wasn't working in the diningroom, I didn't get the opportunity to meet the clientele. But one day a guest came into the kitchen and handed me £2 cash as a tip. She was staying in the hotel with mime artiste Marcel Marceau's entourage and she had heard me singing in the kitchen. She told me I was the happiest dishwasher she had ever heard!

Maura Cullinane, who was a waitress in the hotel, had a car and one day I persuaded her to take me down to Galway where I was applying for a place in the Regional College. It wasn't her day off, so she made an excuse and told them she was going to a wedding. Margaret was off, so she came too. I did the interview and got my place in the college. On the way back we bought a paper and I discovered that the Rose of Tralee festival was on in County Kerry. It was the final night of the event. We looked at each other ... and the next instant we were on the road to Kerry. We had a wonderful evening in Tralee. I remember being smitten by the Jersey 'Rose' – I thought she was gorgeous. We drove back to Dublin through the night and Maura had to put her head out the window to stay awake while driving. I got to bed at 6.30 that morning and I had to be up at 7.30 again to get the bus to work. On the journey in to the hotel I thought I was going to get sick, I was so tired.

That was the summer I also learned how to drive. Maura taught me in her own little blue Ford Fiesta. I remember, God bless us and save us, didn't she let me drive from Dublin to Glendalough in County Wicklow one day. And I not fit to drive, no more than the cat. And I had no insurance or anything. But that was a good summer for me. Poor Maura is no longer with us; she was a lovely girl. She died in 1992. I'm still very friendly with Margaret and I attended her wedding in 1992. That's something I'm very pleased about, the fact that the people I knew before my career took off are still part of my life today and they still want me in their lives. I'm glad that never changed.

In the autumn of 1980, I set off to Galway city to take up my place in the Regional College. My course was in business studies and my long-term plan was to eventually transfer to university. I had decided at one stage that I wanted to be a teacher. And if my passion for the stage hadn't made me change my direction, I think I would have been a reasonably good teacher. I'm fairly relaxed and hard to ruffle. I'm also very good at communicating with people and that's another reason why I thought I might teach. I didn't get enough points for university in my Leaving Cert., so I was using the Regional College as a stepping stone. It would have taken a bit longer. But sure I had all the time in the world. I was only eighteen.

But my time in Galway Regional College turned out to be

the most unhappy period of my life. I never settled and I was really miserable. I never socialised in the college. I had nothing in common with that kind of life or the people there. To this day, I still have no friends from that centre of education. The friends I made during that era were from outside the college, in particular Sean and Pat Nugent, the family I was staying with. They made me feel really at home and a part of their clan. Pat is the lady who said, 'Wouldn't you be better off learning something first,' when I broke the news to her that I was leaving college to become a singer.

They did their best to help me settle, but it was a lost cause. I was really homesick for Donegal. From early on, I started going into Galway city to buy the Donegal newspaper. The first time I went in to the city, I borrowed a push-bike from the Nugents. But I ended up walking most of the way because I had never cycled in traffic before and I was terrified. I might as well have been on a highway in the States. In the early stages, I started going home to Kincasslagh every third week-end. It was a gruelling journey which took hours and hours. The bus used to take me up to Donegal town, then I'd have to hitch the remaining forty-three miles to Kincasslagh. But even if Kincasslagh had been on another planet I wouldn't have cared. I would still have made the trek. In the end, I was doing that journey every weekend. So, the writing was on the wall.

Coming up to Christmas of that year, my sister Margaret was performing in Galway and I went to see her in the Galway Ryan Hotel where she was staying. I told her I wanted to leave college and become a singer. She advised me to think about it over Christmas. Margaret still recalls how I sent her a Christmas card that year and on it I wrote: 'Remember what I told you? I want to sing NOW!' And I underlined the word now. So, I never returned to college.

The year 1981 was a new beginning for me. It was the start of something that has snowballed beyond my wildest expectations. Margaret had agreed that I could join her band. It's something I'll always be grateful to her for. Getting a start is always the most difficult aspect of anything you want to do. I was lucky – I had my sister to turn to. So she found a place for me in her group.

On 28 January 1981, I stepped out on stage at a venue called The Rag, in Thurles, County Tipperary. I was on rhythm guitar, but it wasn't plugged in! It wasn't connected to the power because I couldn't play a note. Isn't that dreadful? But sure I had to start somewhere. And if playing a 'dead' guitar was going to kick off my career, then I had no problem with that. Some people start by cleaning offices in Nashville, washing floors or waiting on tables. Maybe standing on a stage with a guitar that's not plugged in isn't as honest as washing floors or waiting on tables, but it gave me the start. I'm sure the other band members must have thought I was a bit of a flute. Anyway, I stuck with it. The guitar, incidentally, belonged to Margaret and she had never learned how to play it either. I had gone to guitar classes, but my heart was never in it. I think I had decided in my mind that if I ever mastered the guitar, I would always be left in the background and I'd never make it out to centre stage as a singer. That first night walking out on stage was a tremendous feeling. I was really excited and a bit giddy. It was wonderful. I was on my way. I felt like Engelbert Humperdinck.

Working with Margaret and her band gave me a wonderful insight into the live music business. It was great experience for me. I saw a lot of things that were good. But I also observed a side of the business that I didn't like, such as boozing into the early hours of the morning after a show. There were a lot of things like that that I wouldn't be interested in. And I do believe that what I witnessed with Margaret has made me the way I am. Margaret has had a hard time in her own career because of an alcohol problem, which she has talked about publicly herself. And I knew I never wanted that to happen to me. So many people in this business become victims to drink. It's one of the hazards of the scene. I never wanted to drink. And I think my mother was the main reason for that. She drummed it into us not to drink.

But on the positive side, I saw the joy that Margaret brought to people. And I saw how people admired her. And I wanted all those things too. Margaret allowed me to share the limelight on stage when she gave me a turn at the singing. Eventually, I was performing seven or eight songs during the night. I suppose I always got a good response. But I remember one night in particular, it was in the St Francis Club in Birmingham, I sang 'My Donegal Shore' and I can still recall the applause. It was the first time that it really hit me. I knew then I was making an impression. It must have struck Margaret too, because she got me to sing a verse and chorus of the song again. Inevitably, the time came for me to move on and spread my wings. I had to leave Margaret in order to progress. My final performance as a member of my sister's band was in the Longford Arms Hotel in Longford town on 27 April 1983.

My Donegal Shore and The Miracle

The song that started the ball rolling for me in my own career was 'My Donegal Shore'. That composition will always be close to my heart. A guy called Johnny McCauley wrote it. He also wrote the number, 'Pretty Little Girl From Omagh'. Big Tom recorded 'My Donegal Shore' long before me. But the first time it touched a chord with me was when I heard a girl called Bridie Cahill singing it unaccompanied. While it was a slow burner for me, once it took off it certainly shot my career into top gear. I recorded that song with my own money in Big Tom's studios in Castleblaney, County Monaghan, on 9 February 1983. I was always a great saver, a real magpie. And I had accumulated just over £1,000. It cost me £600 to record it on tape and it took another £600 to release it on record. That was the best money I ever spent. My sister, Kathleen, and her husband, John, drove me up to Castleblaney that day and in the evening I left with a little tape which had four tracks on it: 'My Donegal Shore', 'Stand Beside Me', 'London Leaves' and 'Married By The Bible' (that one never escaped at all!). In the studio that day, I remember thinking: 'What am I doing here? What do these people think of me?' I suppose I was insecure at the time. I knew why I was doing it, but I didn't really know what I was doing. I do remember the fella who was producing it – Basil Hendrix, an English musician who lives in Ireland – saying, 'That chap can sing.'

I opted for 'My Donegal Shore' and 'Stand Beside Me' on the record and I put it out on Margaret's label. I then sold every one of those records myself. I sold them anywhere and everywhere. I even sold them on a pilgrimage to Knock shrine in County Mayo, where the Blessed Virgin once appeared. I sang on the bus all the way down and all the way back and the pilgrims bought the records from me. Annie McGarvey bought one and she didn't even have a record player! In all, I had a thousand records and I sold all of them and that covered my costs. I also sought a few people's advice on it. One of the individuals I approached was a country music radio critic. His comment was, 'Well, it's nice, but there's nothing spectacular about it.' I was disgusted by his reaction. Sometime later, I met him coming out of a bank in Dublin's College Green and I was tempted to confront him and give him a piece of my mind. I was so determined to make it that anybody who didn't say, 'Yes, you can do it,' I pushed aside. I almost hated them. Nothing or nobody was going to get in my way.

Scotland was my first attack. I had friends in Glasgow – Kathleen and Eugene Sweeney. Whenever I stayed with them, they used to take me down to The Claddagh Club, The Irish Centre and The Squirrel Bar. Invariably, I got up to sing in those venues. So, when I brought out the record, I went over in May and it was arranged with the owners or managers of the venues that I could sing and that we could sell my records, which I brought along in a hold-all. I sang the songs which were on the single and Kathleen sold them to the audience. I went down so well that the three venues invited me back to sing with their resident band. So I went back to Glasgow for a weekend and that was the first time I was advertised as a singer in my own right. And once I got my name up in lights, I never took it down.

In July 1983, I got my first band together: Daniel O'Donnell and Country Fever. It featured Patrick Gallagher and Peter Healy (now with an Irish band, Goats Don't Shave), Dim

Breslin and Joe Rogers, all of whom were from my area. And our first night was in The Ostan Hotel in Dungloe. I'll never forget it. I had the whole repertoire sung by 1 a.m. and we were booked to play till 2 o'clock in the morning. So, I started the first number again and off we went. We continued playing around our own area. When most bands are starting off, members come and go, and we were no exception. Patrick Gallagher and Dim Breslin left and my friend P.J. Sweeney joined, along with Joe Rogers and his brother Peter. We went over to Scotland and did the same venues in Glasgow and then we went down to England and played in The Boston Club, Tufnell Park, The Forresters in Tooting, The Manor House in Manor House, all in London, and The Irish Centre in Leeds. That band stayed together until April 1984.

We got great support from people outside the business. People like Anne Breslin and Ann Birrane, who used to secure dates for us in London. I first met Ann Birrane when I was in Margaret's band. She's a wonderful lady – she would even send me the fare to come over and do the shows. And the six of us used to stay with Anne Breslin and her husband in Archway Road. It was always people outside showbusiness who gave me support in the early days.

A woman called Nan Moy was managing my sister Margaret when I was a member of her band. Nan and I always got on well together, so when she was parting company with Margaret, we decided we'd start a band together. That turned out to be The Grassroots and we launched it on 15 June 1984. The Grassroots featured Gerard Gallagher, Larry Gallagher, Gerry Flynn, Roy Campbell, Jimmy Hussey and Tommy Shanley. But two days before our first performance, we were having problems getting an official line-up together. In fact, we didn't have a band. So I phoned Jim The Cope, who was organising the dance, to tell him there was no way we could start on the Friday. Jim revealed that he had already advertised the group and we would have to play. If he had said he'd cancel it I might never have restarted, because everything seemed to be going wrong at that point. Between the jigs and the reels, we got a band together for the night. I remember being down in Dublin trying to organise it. I was virtually broke. I was staying with my brother James, so I didn't have the expense of accommodation. But on one of the days I was out around the city and I was faced with the choice of having a Big Mac and chips in McDonald's and walking home, or just having chips and getting the bus home. I'm totally addicted to McDonald's, so I ended up walking home.

The band I eventually rustled up for the night was like James Last's, it was so big, except that one half didn't know what the other half was doing. There must have been about seven in the group, when there should only have been four. But, I suppose there was safety in numbers. We got through the night and there was a good crowd at the venue. Then we went down to Kerry the next night and there was nobody in the place. But that was a regular experience in the early days. There would often be more people on the stage than on the dancefloor. But I never 'died' on stage. Even the night we only had six people. I recall playing down in Julian's of Midfield, County Mayo, one night and there were only a half-dozen people there. I put on a great show, even if I do say so myself. And John Julian said to me later, 'Do you know, if you don't succeed there's no justice.' I remember those words.

Like every band, I had my share of experiences on the road during those early days. There were lots of long journeys in the back of a van. And the most bizarre incident happened on a trip from England to Scotland. At the time, I had a van which

I bought in Dublin and which ran on petrol and gas. During the journey there was a big bang and I thought the gas was blowing up. We stopped and jumped out of the wagon, but everything seemed to be okay. We continued on down the road and the van started heating up. There was no water in it. So they all looked at me.

'What are you going to do?'

'What am I going to do?' And me knowing nothing about vans and engines.

We had no water. It was pouring out of the heavens. We were on the motorway. We'd go a bit. We'd stop. The van would cool down. Off we'd go again. It would heat up again.

'What are you going to do?'

'What am I going to do?'

So, I called on the boyo up above, Saint Anthony, a man I always had great faith in. I said: 'Now, me boy, this is a crucial point. It's now or never.' Soon after that we approached roadworks and in the distance I could see a hut. I told the driver to pull up and we got out. It was a workman's hut and the big padlock was open and hanging on the door. We went in and there in the middle of that hut was a big five-gallon jar of water! That was a miracle to me because that's exactly what I needed at that time. It's an experience I'll never forget. I suppose St Anthony knew he was gone if he didn't come up trumps that time.

There were times when the six of us had to sleep in the back of the van. On another occasion, the whole lot of us stayed in what they called a family room in a service station. It cost £24 for the gang of us and I said to the woman, 'Does it matter if we don't have a mother with us?' There were lots of long journeys in those days. I always found the trip from Manchester to London and Belmullet to Dublin the most gruelling. But I never really hated the travelling because I always knew there was something good at the end of it. THE STAGE.

Nan Moy was more than just a manager. She was also a good friend. And she tried extra hard, with sometimes very little results. We survived – just about. I remember one night I had spent hours in a car travelling hundreds of miles to a venue outside Charleville, County Cork, and I got there to find only a handful of people at the dance. It was a big, long dancehall and I could see my friend Josephine down at the door collecting the cash because there were so few in the place. On the way back, we spent the money in a Kentucky Fried Chicken take-away. That was typical of how it was in those days. We did, in turn, perform in places like The Gresham and The National ballrooms in London and stuffed them. From 1984 into 1985, we were doing a roaring trade in big venues around England, but nothing was happening for us in Ireland.

In 1985, I performed at the Irish Festival in London. I had also performed there in 1982 with Margaret and I remember thinking on that occasion, 'I'd love to top the bill here some day.' Ten years later my dream came true. But my performance there in 1985 was instrumental in getting me noticed by the 'right' people. Not that I was aware of it. For some time, a man called Bill Delaney of I and B Records in England had been telling Ritz Records boss, Mick Clerkin, about 'this fella called Daniel O'Donnell who is causing a ripple'. And I remember somebody saying to me at that time: 'You should be with Mick Clerkin. Ritz is the company for you.' Ritz had already done great things for Foster and Allen and The Fureys, giving them pop chart success. Both acts even appeared on 'Top of the Pops', which had a huge impact at the time. I knew that Mick Clerkin would be a tremendous asset to have behind me, but my feeling was, 'Sure why would he be bothered with me?'

But fortune smiled upon me and when I did the Irish Festival in 1985, Mick was there. It turned out to be one of my best performances. I got a great reaction. Mick saw it and he contacted me. He offered me the chance to record an album with Ritz and the result was *The Two Sides Of Daniel O'Donnell*, which was released in the autumn of 1985. Prior to that, I had already recorded an album, *The Boy From Donegal*. It featured 'My Donegal Shore', 'The Old Rustic Bridge', 'Galway Bay', 'Forty Shades Of Green', 'My Side Of The Road', '5,000 Miles From Sligo', 'The Old Bog Road', 'Slievenamon', 'Noreen Bawn', 'Ballyhoe', 'Home Is Where The Heart Is' and 'Shutters And Boards'.

Nan Moy was still my manager at that time. But I knew that Nan and I were never going to make it together. We had already spent a lot of money and we might as well have been flushing it down a loo, because we were never going to get it back the way we were going. So, I was faced with probably one of the hardest decision I've ever had to make in my life. On Friday, 13 December 1985 – and I'm superstitious – I remember stopping in Ballisodare, County Sligo, on the way to a venue and phoning Mick Clerkin for an appointment. I had decided to part company with Nan Moy. And I was hoping to persuade Ritz to take over total control of my career. I made my decision in Manchester at the beginning of December. Coming out of the Ardree Club, I said to Loretta Flynn, who is now my Fan Club secretary and general assistant, 'This isn't working.' The thought of giving it all up and doing something else even crossed my mind. I didn't realise that the record 'My Donegal Shore' was getting airplay and gaining momentum. I didn't realise that the local radio stations were picking up on it.

I went to see Mick Clerkin and, to my amazement, he was

interested in me. He didn't know what arrangement I had with Nan, whether or not I would part company with her. But I knew then what I had to do. I told Nan that it wasn't working; that Ritz were interested in me and that I was leaving her. It was a dreadful decision to have to make. At the time, Nan was naturally upset over it and it took her a little time to accept it. It definitely put a strain on our friendship, but only for a short time. Nan knows now, as she did shortly afterwards, that it was for the best. And we are still great friends. She is very much a part of my life and I'm delighted with that because in our day we had some great times on the road while we struggled to overcome the seemingly endless obstacles that we encountered. Today, we can look back and laugh at some of the experiences we had. Like the day she phoned me to tell me that the van had been lifted [repossessed] because we couldn't make the repayments. It was the day before one of our shows in Manchester.

'Sure we can hire another van for the show,' I said, unperturbed by this latest catastrophe to befall the band.

But there was even worse news. 'The gear was in the van and that's been lifted too,' she replied.

Now, THAT was problem. But you become very enterprising when you're in a struggling band and living hand-to-mouth. Ronnie and I decided to go over on the plane and link up with some of the musicians in the resident band there. So we headed off with only an accordion and a string machine. We were like Laurel and Hardy. But we got by on the night, playing with the resident group in Manchester. Then we had to go on to Newcastle, where we teamed up with a guitarist and a drummer for the show. The only song in the whole repertoire that the guitar player knew was 'It's A Long Way To Tipperary'. I don't know how we did it, but we did manage to get through that night, too. We told the people in both venues that the reason we couldn't bring over our full band was due to the fact that the back axle had fallen out of the van. We couldn't tell them the real story. Mind you, the back axle had previously fallen out, so we weren't telling a lie, we were just stretching the truth a little!

Then there was the time that Nan and I went down to Dublin to pick up the first ever colour posters that we had printed for advertising our shows. I suppose that was a big day in my career then. My own colour posters. On the way back through Donegal, we got a puncture on the Gweebarra bends, a stretch of road between Maas and Leiter. It was dark. It was wet. It was windy. At the time, I hadn't a clue how to change a wheel. Even to this day, changing a wheel is still a major ordeal for me. I opened the boot of the car and a whole load of the posters blew away across the fields. Then, Nan had safety nuts on the wheel and I couldn't get them off. It was a nightmare. Those sorts of things happened on a regular basis. But nowadays we can look back on them and fall around the place laughing.

I finished up with Nan and the band in January 1986 and went off the road.

THE SECOND COMING

As the bells rang out on New Year's Eve, heralding the arrival of 1986, and the frenzied celebrations got into full swing, I was quietly pondering the year ahead. I was really snapping at my last bite of the showbiz cherry. If my new association with Ritz didn't work out, then it was the end of the road for me. I was twenty-four years old and life was passing me by. By this stage, most of my friends from school were engaged in secure jobs. Some of them were married and had started a family. Their lives were blossoming out along the traditional route. But I still had nothing to show for all my hard work. I didn't even have a car. I had no money. Worse than that, I was up to my neck in debt. As far as I was concerned, I had made absolutely no headway in my drive to establish my name as a singer. My life was really in tatters and it was make-or-break time. But I hadn't contemplated a life away from the stage. I wasn't qualified to do anything else. I couldn't even play a musical instrument. My future certainly looked very bleak indeed if the year ahead didn't bear some fruit. It began to dawn on me that I might have to take the emigrant boat or plane, like a multitude of my fellow countrymen and women and start a new life in America or far-away Australia.

It was with a certain amount of trepidation then that I began my relationship with Ritz Records and with the man behind the successful company, Mick Clerkin. When I look back now, I realise that I had absolutely no concept of the huge network of contacts and expertise that Ritz would employ to launch Daniel O'Donnell. I knew they had been very successful with other artistes. But, I suppose I never put it down to the record company, I probably attributed it to the artistes themselves. Foster and Allen, Davey Arthur and The Fureys were already big names when they joined Ritz, so I believed that had something to do with the success they achieved after they joined the company. On the other hand, I was virtually unknown and I hadn't achieved any success worth talking about.

Looking back over my life, it's not easy to select the greatest moments or the best experiences. But a guy called Sean Reilly rates among the top of the best things that ever happened to me in my whole life without a shadow of doubt. After I left Nan Moy and joined Ritz, I had no one to take personal control of my career. Ritz had taken responsibility for managing me, but it wasn't possible for Mick Clerkin to run his organisation and give me individual attention. It was at that stage that Sean Reilly came into my life. Sean comes from the same Irish county as Mick Clerkin – they are both Cavan men. And it was Mick who suggested that Sean might be the man for me. He told me that Sean was a professional manager with many years' experience in the business; that he had a great reputation and was highly respected among his peers and that he was a guy I could work well with. I had no idea then that I was going to meet a prince of a man who has become as important to me as any member of my own family. He's a man I trust implicitly with my private as well as my business affairs. Today, Sean Reilly is like a brother and a father to me.

I remember meeting Sean in Dublin's Gresham Hotel at the beginning of 1986. How I wanted so much to create the right impression that day. I didn't know Sean at the time. I had never met him before. But I realised he was the guy who would be rooting for me in my bid for stardom. I knew it would be Sean who would be working towards the goal that I wanted to achieve. So, the day I met him, I wanted him to be impressed with me. I wanted him to see a guy who had potential if only it was harnessed and steered in the right direction. I wanted him to believe in me because I believed in myself. Even though years of hard graft had yielded virtually nothing, I still knew that I had the makings of a top-level performer. Sean is a quiet-spoken man who is very down-to-earth. And I knew instantly that we were going to get on well together. I had a letter one time from a fan who is wheelchair-bound and she paid me a lovely compliment by telling me that I look at her and see a person in a chair, rather than a chair with a person in it. I soon discovered that it's the same with Sean. He sees a person who sings, rather than a singer who is a person. During that meeting, I knew instinctively that he was a man I could trust with my life, as, indeed, I have done. He exudes an understated confidence and I could see that he is good at what he does. I left the hotel that day with a happy heart and a great weight lifted from my shoulders. My life was beginning to come together again.

Mick Clerkin is a man of few words. He doesn't believe in a lot of small talk. He doesn't give you the type of salesman-spiel you get from a lot of guys in this business. His conversation is not peppered with a load of hype. Mick is also down-to-earth – it must be something to do with the laid-back lifestyle around picturesque County Cavan. So, I now had two good men backing me. At the time, however, I didn't realise how much time, effort and financial resources were going to be invested in Daniel O'Donnell. I had absolutely nothing myself. I was still stone broke, not a penny to my name. It was Mick Clerkin who put all the money behind me initially. Of course, he obviously recognised the potential. But nothing is a sure-fire winner, especially in this business. Thank God he had the foresight to go with his gut instinct. A lot of others didn't give me any chance whatsoever. There's hardly a band manager in Ireland who wasn't approached to take me on in the early stages before Ritz. And they all turned me down! I'll never forget one guy's words. He told me, 'Ah, you'll last about six months.' I suppose they all thought that the type of songs that I was singing were outdated, out of fashion and that I was out of my mind if I thought I was ever going to get anywhere with them. Mick Clerkin took a different view and obviously had more foresight. He took a chance on me. And, of course, it's a two-way thing. An empty bag will never look full, no matter what you do with it. I was somebody Ritz could do something with.

I remember hearing about one Irish newspaper article which referred to me as the 'designer bogman'. It was a put-down line, something I have experienced quite a lot from the trendy types in the media in Ireland. I suppose the insinuation is that I'm a brainless mannequin who has been styled and dressed up, then programmed to sing the type of songs that are in my repertoire. Nothing could be further from the truth. It wasn't like that at all with Ritz. There was no physical grooming involved. They didn't try to alter my stage act in any way. Granted, professional photography was employed for my promotional material. But that's a feature of the business that every artiste or group utilises. They did buy me a new wardrobe, simply because I didn't have a great variety of stage gear. They probably sent me to a hairdresser to have my hair styled. I realise that my hair always looks so perfect – not a hair out of place – but that's just the way it is naturally. I don't have to do an awful lot with it. When I go out on stage, it probably looks as if I've spent several hours brushing it. In fact, after I wash and dry it, I just have to run my fingers through it and it's fine. There was no radical grooming by the Ritz people. Mick was obviously happy with the way I performed on stage. And he must have decided not to tamper with my presentation.

The first thing they did, however, was put a band behind me. Around the time that Ritz took me over, a professional Irish band called Jukebox were splitting up. They were signed up by Ritz to be my backing band. Jukebox consisted of Billy Burgoyne, Tony Murray and Pearse Dunne. And I brought Ronnie Kennedy with me. Ronnie and I relate so well together. We have a wonderful understanding. Today, I think that everybody can see that on stage. Sometimes you meet a person and you know that you're going to get on so well together. You also know that he or she is going to be the first person you're going to have a row with. That's the sign of a good friendship. Because someone you never have a row with, you never really have a friendship with either. I realise that now. With Ronnie, I knew there were going to be lots of rows. And we get on like brothers.

From the moment I started on the road as part of the Ritz enterprise, I have never had a bad night. Our first show was on 6 March 1986, in St Cyprian's Club, in Brockley, Kent. There was a good turnout, it was a good show and from there a tornado just swept me along and took me to heights beyond my greatest expectations. For me, the period from January to March 1986, was like getting up in the morning in daylight having gone to bed in the dark. The first couple of months of that year were my dark period. It was a period of uncertainty. But once I got on the road, a whole new world was beginning to open up for me. If any struggling young performer came up to me today and asked me what was the secret ingredient of my success, I still could not put my finger on it. Why did it all suddenly happen for me overnight after I joined up with Ritz? I suppose it was a combination of having a good band and a professional machine behind me. Ritz pulled out all the stops to ensure that everybody knew about me and that I got maximum exposure. I was their 'priority' act and they pumped everything in to 'breaking' me.

One unusual feature of the Irish scene at that time which worked to my advantage was the plethora of pirate radio stations that had captured the imagination of the nation, particularly around rural Ireland. The national music station was then Radio 2. It was primarily a pop and rock station. Up-and-coming singers like myself who were turning out the country and Irish songs didn't get a look in. Disco music had seen to that. It killed off a lot of the live bands in Ireland and the country's once thriving ballrooms were being deserted for the trendy clubs with flashing lights and loud music. From the heady days of the sixties, when a big showband star like Larry Cunningham is often quoted as having remarked, 'I haven't seen floorboards since Christmas,' the ballroom crowds had dwindled to such an extent that there wasn't a dancing foot to raise the dust. Rural ballrooms that once almost burst at the joints because of overcrowding, were now sad, empty shells in the middle of nowhere. And where once upon a time Joe Dolan could be heard belting out 'The Westmeath Bachelor' or 'Tar And Cement', only the sound of the wind whistling in the bushes broke the night silence.

I'm not blaming Radio 2 in Ireland for the demise of that scene. It was just changing trends and fashion. And they had to go with the music of the day to capture the young listeners. I do think, however, that they underestimated the sizeable support that still existed for the type of music that myself and tens of thousands of other people have taken to our hearts. There was still a major following for country music and Irish songs and that soon emerged when the pirate radio stations started mushrooming around Ireland. Suddenly, artistes like myself now had access to the airwaves again. Whereas, on Radio 2 you might be lucky to get a few plays for your record, the pirates would play it several times a day. And that helped to bring Irish artistes to the fore again. It turned them into stars all over again. And I do believe that it rejuvenated the live venues again, as the disco clubs began to lose their gloss. Radio 2 in Ireland, now known as 2FM, has since changed its policy. There are now two special weekend shows featuring country and Irish music, which are presented by Alan Corcoran. And during the week, daily shows also play music by artistes like myself.

I happened to come along at the right time in Ireland. The disco scene had peaked and the pirate radio stations captured a growing market that touched the core of Irish society. They were playing Big Tom. They were playing Philomena Begley. They were playing Margo. Artistes that were already house-hold names. And when they started to play Daniel O'Donnell, people began to sit up and take notice. I was a new name. A new voice. An unknown quantity. There was a curiosity value attached to Daniel O'Donnell. Who is he? Where has he suddenly come from? And I was also the first of a new breed of singers to emerge. Perhaps today it would be more difficult for me to make the same impact? It's a question I can't really answer. But I'm glad that the right set of circumstances came along at that time. I do believe that if you persevere for long enough you will eventually get the rewards you're seeking. Nothing comes easy in this life. You have to get out there and fight for it.

The pirate radio stations right across Ireland had picked up on *The Two Sides Of Daniel O'Donnell*, the album I had recorded with Ritz before the end of 1985. So, the key had

already been turned in the ignition and my engine was begin-
ning to crank up. That album featured: 'The Green Glens Of
Antrim', 'The Blue Hills Of Breffni', 'Any Tipperary Town',
'The Latchyco', 'Home Town On The Foyle', 'These Are My
Mountains', 'My Donegal Shore', 'Crying My Heart Out Over
You', 'My Old Pal', 'Our House Is A Home', 'Your Old Love
Letters', '21 Years', 'Highway 40 Blues' and 'I Wouldn't
Change You If I Could', all of which were capturing the
attention of radio listeners.

Meanwhile, the band was taking a while to settle down, as
new bands do. John Staunton joined in the summer of 1986.
Billy Condon joined in the summer of 1987. Kevin Sheerin and
John Ryan joined in the spring of 1988 and that line-up
remained intact until I was forced to go off the road at the
beginning of 1992. When I resumed my stage performing after
a break of four months, Kevin and John didn't return. They had
decided to pursue other projects. It was an amicable parting
and we are still in contact. John is still my musical arranger,
and in 1992 Kevin returned to the stage with his own group,
The New Hillbillies. They were replaced in my band by
Richard Nelson and Raymond McLoughlin.

Every night at the end of a performance, I always take time
out to introduce the individual members of my group to the
audience. And I always tell the people who come to see us
that to me they are the best band in the world. I tell them that
I have tremendous admiration for all the lads. And that's not
just throwaway spiel. Perhaps, when you say something like
that at the end of each show it becomes meaningless. But my
tribute to the lads is quite sincere. I really do mean what I say.
I would be nothing today if it wasn't for the people who support
me. My show would be nothing without the contribution from
my band. It's not just me out there on stage doing all the work.

Without a good band behind me it would be a totally different show. And most of the lads have been with me from the day I joined Ritz and together we have watched something incredible come to life.

We started off attracting big crowds. We weren't playing to full houses immediately. But it wasn't long before the queues started to form outside venues around Ireland. This was a totally new phenomenon. It was reminiscent of the old Irish showband days back in the 'swinging sixties' when the ballrooms were in full flight, struggling to cope with the crowds that created the sweaty atmosphere. And I do believe that once the 'bush telegraph' started spreading the word that this new guy Daniel O'Donnell was something of a sensation, it had a knock-on effect. I was now a curiosity item and more and more people started coming out to see what all the fuss was about. Maybe initially they came along for that reason, but I was obviously doing something right because they kept on coming back again and again and again ...

I don't think I was aware of the full extent of my drawing power at that time. I didn't dwell on it. I was just happy to see lots of people at my shows. But there were thousands of people coming to see us. And people kept telling me, 'It's like the old showband days.' I wasn't thinking along those lines because I was never a part of the old ballroom days. I had heard about it. I had read about it. But it was before my time. And I wasn't conscious of the fact that I was creating a whole new dancing scene in Ireland again. I didn't realise that I was introducing a new generation to the joy of dancing to the sound of a live band on stage. And I suppose it was a new experience for some of them. I think the first time I consciously started to notice the crowds was in 1986 when we performed in Dungiven in the north of Ireland. The band would arrive at the venue at seven o'clock in the evening to set up their gear and a queue would already be forming outside. When I heard that I thought it was quite incredible, because our show didn't start until eleven o'clock. In the early stages, I was much more popular in the North and, consequently, I was attracting bigger crowds there. But I soon began to see the same trend developing in the Republic. The first time I noticed it there was when we played in Enniskean, County Cork. This was our second visit. We had had a reasonably large crowd the first time, but on the second time back it was packed. That soon became the norm right across the country.

The Two Sides Of Daniel O'Donnell established me as a recording artiste. It brought me a long way in Ireland and got people familiar with the type of material that is now my trademark. But it was the follow-up album, *I Need You*, which helped to launch my career in Britain. Throughout my years in showbiz, I have encountered some really bizarre coincidences and experiences. And one of them involved that song, 'I Need You'. One night we were playing in a venue called The Georgian, in Ballina, County Mayo, and a fan called Anne, whom I had known for some time, came up to me. She started talking about this song from the sixties that her sister liked and she suggested that it would be my type of song. So, I asked her to send it on to me. One day it arrived in the post. She had recorded it on to a tape, obviously from an old record because it was quite noisy and crackly. The moment I played it I knew that it did suit me and I loved it. The strange thing about that song is, when I took it down to Ritz in Dublin to suggest recording it, Mick Clerkin already had it in his possession. He had picked it up from a totally different source during the same period and he was going to suggest it to me as a suitable song! I still find that very strange. It's as if some supernatural force has had a hand in steering my career.

I recorded the album *I Need You* towards the end of 1986 and in addition to the title track, it featured: 'Sing An Old Irish Song', 'From A Jack To A King', 'Lovely Rose Of Clare', 'Stand Beside Me', 'Irish Eyes', 'Dear Old Galway Town', 'Three Leaf Shamrock', 'Veil Of White Lace', 'Kickin' Each Other's Hearts Around', 'Medals For Mothers', 'Wedding Bells', 'Snowflakes', 'Your Friendly Irish Way', 'Lough Melvin's Rocky Shore' and 'I Love You Because'. When Ritz started promoting that album in Britain, the reaction to it was very favourable and it started to move.

In the spring of 1987, I went to Inverness, Scotland, to perform in The Eden Court theatre for the first time. For some reason, I always wanted to sing in the north of Scotland. I remember seeing Inverness in a tour brochure of Irish country singer, Susan McCann, and I instantly became attracted to it. So Inverness was always on my mind as a place to perform and going there was the realisation of yet another dream. Now Inverness is very special to me because it was there that I got my first ever standing ovation. It took me completely by surprise when the audience stood up at the end and clapped for several minutes. It was something I had never experienced before. And I didn't know how to respond to it. I remember thinking, 'I should be doing something special now to justify this.' But apart from a somersault, there was nothing more I could do.

The Theatre Royal in Norwich, England, is another venue that will always be special to me. It was in Norwich that I performed to a predominantly English audience for the first time. I'll never forget that night. I was so nervous. I suppose it was fear of the unknown. I had performed in England many times before that, but this was different. On the previous trips over, I had played Irish venues, with an Irish audience and I was fairly relaxed because I was confident that they would be familiar with the songs. Norwich was going to be a different scene altogether. When I arrived at the venue, my first question to the promoter Dick Condon was, 'Will there be many Irish people at the show?' And the reply I got was, 'About ten percent.' My heart sank into my stomach. Oh, holy God, I thought, how am I going to survive the night at all? I went out to the wings that night to see the 'warm up' band perform – they were English – and my reaction was, 'I'll never be as good as that!' But eventually my turn arrived and I went out and started into my show. Once I found myself on stage I was fine. And, to my surprise, the audience gave me an enthusiastic response and took me to their hearts. I realised then that there was more to Irish music, that it didn't just appeal to Irish people. Before I went to Norwich, I hadn't even heard of the place. I didn't know it existed. Years later, I told the audience there that way back then I thought Norwich was a building society! The song, 'I Need You', is the one that the people in both Inverness and Norwich were familiar with. It's the one that opened the swinging doors for me right across Britain. Thanks, Anne! I have done many concert tours covering Scotland, England and Wales and I'm always well received. The enthusiasm of the audience has never diminished. It still remains a mystery to me. My repertoire doesn't alter to any great extent, yet the people who come to my shows still greet every song with the same degree of affection. Perhaps they regard the songs as old friends? But words can't adequately describe how I feel about the reception I receive on my tours.

In 1987, I recorded the album *Don't Forget To Remember*, which, in addition to the title track, featured the songs: 'I Don't Care', 'Old Loves Never Die', 'I Wonder Where You Are

Tonight?', 'Don't Be Angry', 'Roses Are Red', 'Before I'm Over You', 'Take Good Care Of Her', 'Pretty Little Girl From Omagh', 'Green Willow', 'Don't Let Me Cross Over', 'The Good Old Days', 'Pat Murphy's Meadow' and 'I Just Can't Make It On My Own'. It was also the year that I did my first major festival in Britain.

In the early stages, festivals were a challenge to me. And I wanted to do them. The Peterborough festival was where I made my country music debut in 1987. And it was a huge success for me. It drew attention to me as a performer because of all the publicity surrounding that extravaganza and it helped to get me noticed by an even wider audience. In October 1987, following Peterborough, I embarked on my first major nation-wide UK tour. It was another milestone in my career – performing the concert circuit. While I was apprehensive starting out, I soon relaxed when I saw the response and out of the twenty-two dates, sixteen of them were sell-out shows. My career had now moved into top gear and I was performing in a new league. The sun was really shining on my world. This was what I had always worked towards. Yet, when it happened it seemed too good to be true. It was difficult for me to comprehend how far I had progressed since joining Ritz. I felt it was better not to dwell on it and I just put my head down and kept on working flat out.

When you're struggling, nothing seems to go right. But when you get rolling, everything fits into place. When I was in Inverness, Eamon Leahy, my tour director who has also played a big role in getting my career on the road, came into my dressingroom and told me that the *I Need You* album was going into the British Country Chart at No. 14. At that time, I wasn't even aware that there was a British Country Chart. Wasn't I very naive? My heart skipped a beat with excitement and I went scouring magazines to find the chart. The album went into the Top 10 the following week, 28 March 1987, and at the time of writing (1992), it's still in the Top 10.

Three months later, my earlier album, *The Two Sides Of Daniel O'Donnell* made its chart entry. At the end of August 1987, 'Take Good Care Of Her'/'Summertime In Ireland' made it to the No. 1 spot in the Irish singles charts. That was one of the most exciting experiences of my life. My first No. 1. The Irish charts show, presented by Larry Gogan on Radio 2, was broadcast every Sunday. Ritz had had an indication that the song had gone into the No. 1 position, but I still tuned in to hear the charts that weekend and I was thrilled. Totally elated. It was wonderful. I don't get much satisfaction out of making records – it's something that I have to do and I do it to the best of my ability. But I don't actually enjoy the recording process because there is no audience there to lift you and to bounce off. I miss that. The only fun I get out of making records is watching them perform in the charts. I love the charts. And getting a No. 1 still gives me a kick. The week I had my first No. 1 coincided with my holidays. But I remember how I wanted to sing all that week.

On 31 October, within one week of its release, *Don't Forget To Remember* entered the UK Country Chart at No.1. That achievement certainly took my breath away. I could scarcely believe it. It was like having a fairy godmother wave a magic wand and make all the things that I wished, happen for me. It was a time for celebration right enough. I think it took Ritz completely by surprise, as it did everyone else, because this had all happened in less than two years. My next album, *From The Heart* repeated that achievement on 29 October 1988. It's a sixties album, featuring: 'The Minute You're Gone', 'It Doesn't Matter Anymore', 'Mary From Dungloe', 'Bye Bye

Love', 'The Old Rugged Cross', 'Wasting My Time', 'Kelly', 'Things', 'Act Naturally', 'Honey', 'Wooden Heart', 'It Keeps Right On A'Hurting', 'My Bonnie Maureen', 'I Know That You Know', 'Old Dungarvan Oak' and 'Danny Boy'. *From The Heart* also crossed over into the British pop charts where it remained for twelve weeks. I'd say that had U2 worried for a while!

The year 1988 marked another landmark in my career when I performed at the Wembley Country Music Festival. That was always a big event, attracting the legendary country music stars from America. My first trip to Wembley was in 1979, when I went over to see Kitty Wells. Kitty was the first female country singer in America to sell a million records with her hit, 'It Wasn't God Who Made Honky Tonk Angels.' That visit to the Wembley festival was a real thrill. It was thronged with people and there was a great atmosphere. I didn't imagine then that one day I would be sharing that same limelight. It was a great sensation.

I also made my Nashville debut in 1988, when I represented Ireland at Fanfare, the showcase for international country music artistes. I sang 'Take Good Care Of Her', 'Don't Let Me Cross Over' and 'Don't Be Angry' before an audience of fifteen thousand and I was very happy with the reaction. The backing group was the legendary Jordanaires, who had performed with 'The King', Elvis Presley. But I suppose the most exciting aspect of that trip was my performance at Nashville's famous Grand Ole Opry, as guest of George Hamilton IV. The country boy from Donegal on stage at the Grand Ole Opry! It was hard to take it all in. The following day, I took the stage at Summer Lights, Nashville's annual four-day street festival, with concert platforms erected in six downtown locations and many of country music's top entertainers performing. I appeared on an open stage outside the Nashville Courthouse – I mustn't have murdered the country songs because they didn't lock me up! – and I shared the bill with George Hamilton IV, Lorrie Morgan and Ricky Skaggs, which was a great honour. A couple of nights later, I was invited to appear at the prestigious Stockyards nightspot by the owner, music publishing magnate Buddy Killan, and I got a very enthusiastic response to my four-song set.

We returned to Nashville six months later and I was invited to perform on the famous 'Nashville Now' TV show, which is televised throughout the United States and Canada and is hosted by top personality, Ralph Emery. It was during this visit that I began working with top record producer Allen Reynolds, who has been responsible for hits by such artistes as Don Williams, Crystal Gayle, Kathy Mattea and Garth Brooks. And from our very first meeting I knew I was going to get on well with Allen. Work on my Nashville album *The Last Waltz* got underway, but in the meantime, I released two new albums, *Thoughts Of Home* and *Favourites* which also headed straight for that top spot in Britain. Wasn't I lucky to find the secret magnet in those charts! *Thoughts Of Home* had: 'My Shoes Keep Walking Back To You', 'Mountains Of Mourne', 'London Leaves', 'Blue Eyes Crying In The Rain', 'Old Days Remembered', 'Send Me The Pillow You Dream On', 'Moonlight And Roses', 'A Little Piece Of Heaven', 'Far Far From Home', 'Isle Of Innisfree', 'My Heart Skips A Beat', 'I Know One', 'I'll Take You Home Again Kathleen', 'Second Fiddle', 'My Favourite Memory' and 'Forty Shades Of Green'. The album *Favourites* featured: 'Bed Of Roses', 'Forever You'll Be Mine', 'Excuse Me (I Think I've Got A Heartache)', 'Halo Of Gold', 'The Streets Of Baltimore', 'Geisha Girl', 'Life To Go', 'That's A Sad Affair', 'Bringing Mary Home', 'Home Sweet Home', 'The Banks Of

Left: A prince of a man! My manager, Sean Reilly, pictured with an exhausted Daniel after my 1990 show in the Sabre Room, Chicago.
Below: My band from 1988 to 1992: John Ryan, Kevin Sheerin, Billy Burgoyne, John Staunton, Ronnie Kennedy, Tony Murray and Billy Condon.

Above: A performance at The Playhouse Theatre, Edinburgh, one of my favourite venues.
Below: There is nothing to compare with what the stage gives me.

Above: I'm in heaven...performing with Loretta Lynn. Right: A night at The Eden Court, Inverness, Scotland.

Above: My favourite portrait.
Left: That's my boy! My Fan Club secretary Lorreta Flynn.

Top: The Nashville 'cowboy'.
Above: Two of the ladies in my life – my mother and sister, Margaret [Margo].

Above: At home with the clan. Back row: My nephew John Francis, brother-in-law John Doogan, niece Patricia, your's truly, sister-in-law Brigid, brother John and nephew Frankie. Front: My sister Kathleen, mother, nephew Daniel, Margaret [Margo], niece Fiona and nephew Joey.

Below: The colleagues who keep me in order when I'm touring: Joe Collum [driver and organiser], Loretta Flynn [Fan Club secretary] and Jim Rosie [compere].

I sing at midnight Mass every Christmas in our local church.

Above: Eddie Rowley, chief showbiz writer with Irish Sunday newspaper SUNDAY WORLD, who worked with me on this book.

Above: Back to school – Belcruit national school where I was a you scholar.

Above: The Cope general store in Kincasslagh where I worked during my schooldays.

My Own Lovely Lee', 'Home Is Where The Heart Is', 'Dublin In The Rare Ould Times' and 'The Green Hills Of Sligo'. Both albums also entered the pop charts and *Thoughts Of Home* was named as Britain's 1989 Country Album Of The Year at the *Music Week* Awards, the UK's weekly music industry publication.

I was very apprehensive about going to Nashville to work. An Irish guy going over to record country songs in the home of country! It was a bit like taking snow to Alaska. I had already met Allen Reynolds and I felt comfortable with him. But I didn't know what people would expect of me. I didn't know what they were going to think of me. How are they going to react to somebody coming from Ireland and singing country music in the way that I do? But I wasn't long in their presence till I felt at home. The people out there are very warm. It turned out to be a really good period for me. I wasn't known out there and I enjoyed the freedom that that gave me. I enjoyed the quiet- ness. I suppose it gave me time to reflect to some extent on the whirlwind that had propelled me through my career since joining Ritz.

Nashville, however, didn't live up to my expectations. Before going there the first time I had this image of legendary country singers strolling down the streets and shows featuring major country stars being staged all over town. But it's not like that at all. In fact, there is very little evidence of country music there. There are no shows, apart from the Grand Ole Opry. Instead, all you find are insurance company offices all over the place, and churches and bible meetings.

But it was a real honour working with a producer of Allen Reynolds' calibre. He's one of Nashville's best-known produc- ers, having caught public attention by turning out international hits for Don Williams and Crystal Gayle in the early and mid-1970s. Over the years he has continued to create some of the most attractive records to come out of the Nashville studios. He's also the guy behind Garth Brooks, who has taken the world by storm. Because both of us had very heavy commitments, our recording work together was done at different stages. The first recording sessions at Allen's Jack's Tracks Studios (on Nashville's 16th Avenue South), were done during May 1989. The second set took place in February 1990. I never intended to do an all-country album, but it was good for me to do it at that time. And I was very happy with the end result. The title for *The Last Waltz* album is derived from the very popular song included on it, 'Last Waltz Of The Evening', which was written by an Irish-based American, Tom Pacheco. I picked it up when I was doing my TV show in Ireland. We invited songwriters to send us their material and we used one song on the show every week and that was one of them. When I heard it first, it didn't really connect with me. But I knew almost immediately that it was for me when I started to sing it. It's a very good song that has become a standard in my live repertoire.

I feel I made a reasonably good impression in Nashville during my visit and I have laid the foundations for further work there. Allen Reynolds is certainly on my side and that can't be bad. He made some very complimentary remarks about me on a late-night 2FM radio show in Ireland, hosted by the Irish showbiz chaplain, Fr Brian D'Arcy, who is also a journalist and broadcaster and was one of the first people to give me media exposure in the *Sunday World*, Ireland's largest-selling national newspaper, when I was starting off. Allen Reynolds did a phone link-up with Brian from Nashville, while I was in the studio in Dublin. And Allen told the listeners that he liked my singing style and he described it as a 'clean, open singing style'. He said he respected me as a performer and he was impressed by my sense of songs, my commitment to the audience and my joy in performing. And far from knocking Irish performers who sing country songs, Allen told Brian that he always felt there was a common link between Irish music and country music. Allen certainly knows how to make a guy feel good!

When *The Last Waltz* eventually came out, it repeated the success of my other albums, going straight to No.1 in Britain's country chart, as well as entering the pop chart. *The Last Waltz* featured: 'Here I Am In Love Again', 'We Could', 'Last Waltz Of The Evening', 'When Only The Sky Was Blue', 'Heaven With You', 'You Know I Still Love You', 'Talk Back Trembling Lips', 'The Shelter Of Your Eyes', 'When We Get Together', 'Ring Of Gold', 'A Fool Such As I', 'Memory Number One', 'Look Both Ways', 'Little Patch Of Blue' and 'Marianne'. In 1991, *The Last Waltz* was voted top album by the British country music magazine *Country Music People*, who also voted me top male vocalist. And Britain's 'Country Music Round Up' voted me most popular male vocalist that year. Another award which I treasure is the one I received in 1989 when I was voted Ireland's Entertainer Of The Year. It's always a great honour and a great thrill to receive that kind of recognition in your own country.

In 1991 I unwittingly became embroiled in a controversy after I was dropped from the UK Country Chart when the chart's supervisory committee decided to re-define country music and ruled that I wasn't 'pure' country. Six of my albums were dropped, because they were considered 'easy listening', rather than country. Well, there was an almighty hullabaloo over that decision. I never realised my fans could be so outspoken. (Incidentally, 'fans' is not a term I like, but I suppose there's no other word to describe them.) They bombarded the British Country Music Association with letters of protest. And I was also really chuffed by the fact that all the regional radio stations in Britain supported me in a vigorous fashion and voiced their outrage over the move. The furore over the charts raged for weeks and made the headlines in newspapers at home and abroad. It was also discussed on radio and television. I was a little embarrassed by all the fuss. They say that there's no such thing as bad publicity, but in the end it was all getting a bit too much for me. And when the Country Music Association finally reviewed the situation and decided after four months to reverse their decision, I was more than relieved. I don't know what effect it would have had on my career in the long term if I hadn't been allowed back into the country chart. But it definitely didn't do me any damage during the short period that it lasted. If anything, it only increased my profile and probably helped to win me a lot more support. I'm very grateful to the fans, the media and everyone who supported me during that saga.

I suppose it is hard to define the type of music that I do. But I do believe it leans more to country than anything else. I know that many of the songs are middle-of-the-road too. I never record material on the basis that it might be a commercial success for me. That's not the way I operate. And while Ritz might come up with songs that they would select as a possible chart hit, they never, ever put pressure on me to record anything I don't want to do. My only rule of thumb is that I will only record a song that I like. So, I suppose all my albums are my own personal favourites. Songs come to me through different channels. I have already described how I picked up 'I Need You' from a fan. And it was Mick Clerkin who found my second No. 1 hit record, 'My Shoes Keep Walking Back To You'. He heard it one night when he was in Nashville. The flip side of that record was 'Far Far From Home', which was written by a County Cavan man, Hugh Donoghue. Irish songwriters in general have been very good for me. I like Hugh's material. He also wrote 'Eileen', which is on the *Best Of* album. His songs suit me and I know I will record more of his work.

Mary Sheridan is another Irish songwriter whose material I like and one of her songs, 'Letter From The Postman's Bag', is also included on the *Best Of* album. I'm also a fan of the work of John Farry from County Fermanagh. He wrote 'Summertime In Ireland', which is on the flip side of my first Irish No. 1 hit. And he's the songwriter who penned 'Lough Melvin's Rocky Shore (*I Need You* album). Songwriters send me material all the time and I go through the different numbers. Sometimes I find something I like. Sometimes I don't. People are always suggesting songs to me. Even the well-known Irish singer and songwriter Christy Moore has helped me out in that department. He came back from Australia with a song for me, which was very kind of him. And then there are all the old songs that I've known for years and that I want to record eventually. I look at songs in a personal way. I have to like the sound and the way it flows. The majority of the songs that I do are very, very simple. They have a simple story. They don't demand a lot of attention and you don't need a dictionary to understand them.

In the days when a lot of the old songs were written, there was no such thing as a video. But now we're in the age of high-technology and the video has certainly made a huge impact on the music industry. In the pop world, it's the video that can often make the song a hit. And there are very few homes nowadays that don't have a little video machine sitting under their telly. So Daniel O'Donnell, of course, has had to make videos too. Whether I like it or not, people want them.

They ask for them. The demand is always there. That has been a whole new experience for me. Of the videos that I've recorded so far, I'm very happy with the 'Thoughts Of Home'. It's shot on location in Ireland and I feel that it really captures the beauty of the Irish countryside. There are some wonderful scenes in that video and for people who don't know my country, who have never had the opportunity to visit it, I feel it gives them a good insight. But the video that I like best is 'An Evening With Daniel O'Donnell', which was recorded during a live show in Dundee, Scotland. I feel it is really representative of me as a performer, although I'm more energetic on stage now than when that video was made. My videos have sold exceptionally well and they have all entered the Top 20 pop video charts, alongside the likes of Kylie Minogue, Jason Donovan, Michael Jackson, U2, Prince and Madonna. In the same bed as Madonna. Isn't that something else!

I'm the type of performer who never gets excited about playing particular venues. Venues are not important to me, no matter how prestigious, or how highly regarded by people in the showbiz world. I only ever judge a show by the audience. Because no matter where you perform, it's not worth talking about if you don't have the audience with you. The Grand Ole Opry was special, I do admit, purely because of its historical association with country music. So, whenever I mention venues, it's the audiences that I have encountered in them during my performances that I'm really referring to. Some venues do act as landmarks in my career. 1988 was the year I performed at The Gaiety Theatre in Dublin and that registered a big step up the ladder for me in my own country. The next 'big' venue was the Royal Albert Hall in London. I have no great memory of that night. I can only recall singing 'The Old Dungarvan Oak' and seeing a Chinese family sitting on the left-hand side.

That intrigued me. I don't know where they came from. I don't know what they were doing there. And I have never seen them since that night.

Then, of course, there was Carnegie Hall in New York. Now that sounds really grand, doesn't it? But to me, it's a venue that's only as good as its audience. Getting the opportunity to have my name up in lights at Carnegie Hall had a bigger effect on other people than it did on me. I was delighted, of course, when I learned that I had a show lined up for that venue. But that was six months before I actually played there, so I didn't dwell on it too much. There were a lot of concerts to play before Carnegie Hall and my main concern was the next show. I didn't dismiss everything I had lined up for the six months leading up to it and just live for Carnegie. But when D-day eventually arrived, I began to realise that I was heading into something special. But, on the other hand, there is always the fear that when something is built up so much, is it going to be everything it's cracked up to be? I did Carnegie during a short tour of the States in 1991 and it was a thrill for me.

I got a bit emotional when I went out onto the stage that night for some strange reason. I recall how I told the audience, 'I never thought I'd get the opportunity to say this: welcome to Carnegie Hall.' Then I went straight into a song because I felt I was going to break down. I never thought I'd see the day when that would happen to me. A flood of emotions hit me. I think what happened to me was as a result of seeing a number of people I knew, sitting in the front row. Some friends of mine from home, John and Anna Brennan, who now live in Perth, Scotland, were in New York on holidays and they had secured tickets for the front row. And there were also some people from Liverpool in the front row, Rene, Alison and Joe, who travel to see me perform on a regular basis. I remember asking myself,

'How did I get here?' I think the memories came flooding back from the days when I couldn't get dates in places that I wanted to play back home when I first started out and there was the sudden realisation of just how far I had come. Carnegie Hall. Then I looked down and saw all the familiar faces and my reaction was, 'This is a wonderful night for us.' I became emotional over the fact that I was able to share the experience with people that I knew so well.

TV AND MY IDOL

I have a big problem in Ireland with my image. There's a large section of the Irish population which firmly believes that Daniel O'Donnell is a boring performer who stands in the one spot on stage throughout his entire show. They think I don't move for fear of disturbing my hair or ruffling my clothes! Some of them probably think I'm brain-dead. That I'm some kind of robot who's programmed to sing. These are people who have never been to a Daniel O'Donnell live show. Their impression of me has been formed from my TV appearances. And, in a way I don't blame them for thinking the way they do. I've always felt that television has represented me very badly. It has never adequately projected the type of stage show that I produce. And that's mainly due to the fact that most of my TV exposure has been studio work. I've always felt that the only way I'm going to get through to a new audience on TV, and encourage them to come along and see my live performance, is through a recording of one of my stage shows on the road. I know I shouldn't be complaining. There are lots of struggling performers who would welcome the opportunity to do some TV in order to get another step or two up the ladder. And there's no doubt that TV has also served me well in Britain and the States. It was great to get the opportunity to appear on shows like 'Wogan' and Val Doonican's show in the UK and on the likes of 'Nashville Now' in the States. Or the legendary 'Late Late Show' with Gay Byrne in Ireland.

But I always feel that I come across as a wax dummy or a plastic figure. It's very hard to project an overall image of what you're about when you have to operate on one spot in a TV studio. I have never enjoyed doing television. People say to me in Britain, 'Why aren't you on television more often?' But to be honest with you, I don't care if I never go on television again. If I'm asked to do television, I will do it more often than not. But I have no desire to do it. Isn't that dreadful? But that's just the way I am. And I can't help the way I feel. But that stated, it's ironic then that I have been offered an incredible amount of TV. Even to the extent of hosting my own series and interviewing my special guests! That's life, I suppose. The people who crave it never get it. My break into 'big time' TV in Ireland arrived in 1989 when I was asked to host a 'special' show featuring country music. It was called 'Country Comes Home' and it featured one of my favourite American country singers, Charley Pride, a performer I had first seen in action at the Wembley Country Music Festival in 1979. He really inspired me on that occasion, so it was a thrill to work with him on the TV show. The 'special' also saw the appearance of that wonderful mother and daughter duo, The Judds. Despite my reservations about doing it, 'Country Comes Home' was a big success, attracting high ratings and critical acclaim. One break can often lead to another and in my case, I was then offered my own TV series, 'The Daniel O'Donnell Show'.

People who know me well will tell you I'm a cool customer. I'm so laid-back at times, I'm almost stretched out on the ground. That's just the way I am. I don't have to work at it. I don't need any form of therapy or sporting activity or drugs to help me cope with the stress that goes with a high-rolling career. By nature, I can take on an awful lot of pressure and handle it quite well. Doing television work can be very stressful, particularly when it's not your natural environment and it's a totally new set of circumstances to have to handle. Hosting a long-running TV series was a new ball game for me. I basically had to come to terms with a new skill overnight. And even though I don't particularly like the medium, I think I handled it well and did a competent job. The producer and director John McColgan said that I took direction very well. In a newspaper interview he acknowledged that his respect for me had grown throughout the series because I was able to memorise the complex instructions that he dished out and get the lines and actions right first time. I probably do have a photographic memory and I'm very visual. I just have to take one look at the layout of a stage before a show and I know where every item of equipment is situated when I'm performing. So I never have to look at the ground.

'The Daniel O'Donnell Show' was a ten-week series of one-hour shows, featuring over forty national and international guests. They included American stars Loretta Lynn, Lorrie Morgan, Ed Bruce, The Forrester Sisters and Stella Parton. And there was a huge line-up of Irish artistes, including The Dubliners, Foster and Allen, Philomena Begley, Susan McCann, Ray Lynam, Margo, Mary Duff, Dominic Kirwan, Mick Flavin and Bridie Gallagher. I was very happy with the series and it also gave me the opportunity to fulfil a life-long ambition – to perform with my idol, Loretta Lynn, the Coalminer's Daughter.

There are a number of fans whom I meet on a regular basis during my concert tours. Some of them I know well because I encounter them so often, and I find it strange when they're nervous in my presence. Off-stage, I'm no different to anyone else. I don't put on any kind of big act to create an aura around me. I'm just a normal guy, so it really was a mystery to me as to why they react in that way. That is, until the day I met Loretta Lynn, and I became a nervous wreck myself.

I don't know if a person can actually say at the end of their day, 'The best day of my life was ...' I don't know if that is possible. But the day I met Loretta Lynn goes down in my book as one of the highlights of my life. A moment to be treasured forever. I still get goose bumps when I think about it. Loretta Lynn has always been the one country singer that I've been totally devoted to. My love affair with lovely Loretta began the day I was introduced to her music by my sister, Margaret. It's very difficult for me to define exactly what it was about Loretta that plucked at my heart strings above any other country singer. I suppose it's her incredible voice. A voice that makes you pulse with excitement. No other artiste has ever made the same impression on me.

I'll never forget the first time I met Loretta. It was way back in 1984 at the Wembley Country Music Festival. That festival sure does bring back a lot of good memories for me. I remember that I was casually strolling around the merchandise stands between shows – the area was like Grand Central Station and I got carried along in the colourful crowd. I'm a great people-watcher and I was totally engrossed by the different characters, some of whom were dressed as cowboys for the day, while others had come along as Indian chiefs. It's all part of the fun of the occasion, an excuse for otherwise normal people, accountants, solicitors, shop assistants and the like, to act out their harmless fantasies. I hardly noticed the lady who was surrounded by an excited group, with individuals clamouring for her attention. Who was creating all the fuss? As I got closer I realised: My God, it's Loretta Lynn. Right there before my eyes. Almost within touching distance. Loretta Lynn! Loretta Lynn! My heart started pumping like a well-tuned engine. This was the singer I had idolised for years. Loretta Lynn! I was like a child waking up on Christmas morning to find his dream toy beside him. Christmas had arrived early for me.

I wanted to race out and tell the whole of London that Loretta Lynn was in Wembley arena and that she was right there in front of me, signing autographs for people. Loretta Lynn! I had been with some friends from Scotland, but we had become separated in the crowd. So I frantically raced around looking for them. Eventually, I located them near the area where we were seated. I was breathless at this stage and I could only gulp: 'L-L-Loretta Lynn. Loretta L-L-Lynn is out there and she's signing autographs.' I wanted them to see her too. I wanted everyone to see this wonderful woman. I went back to the stand and I just stood there before her in the crowd, mesmerised. I was in a trance-like state. She was still signing autographs. Now, I was never an autograph-hunter, but if getting an autograph was the only way I was going to get closer to Loretta Lynn and, my God, even speak to her, then suddenly I had a huge interest in autographs. But how was I going to compose myself to make the approach? My legs were buckling under me at the very thought of it. It seemed like I was there for hours. And as the time ticked away I was no nearer to getting my act together and I almost let the opportunity slip by. But as she was about to depart, I suddenly found myself racing up to her. And, like a dog chasing a bus, I didn't know what to do when I caught up with her. I just blurted out: 'God, I love you!'

Loretta Lynn turned to me and smiled. She smiled at me, Daniel O'Donnell from Kincasslagh, County Donegal. And she whispered: 'Thank you, honey.' She gave me a kiss and then she was gone. Well, talk about being high, I could have flown without wings! It took me weeks to come down from whatever planet I was on.

In 1988 when I went to Nashville to appear at the Fan Fair extravaganza, I went along to see Loretta Lynn's home which is open to the public. I was still carrying the torch for Loretta. And actually being inside her home was an incredible experience. Touching the table where she had her meals. The chair where she relaxed in the evening when she wasn't away on tours. Now, that's all I touched. Loretta, unfortunately, wasn't home when I called. But when I returned to Ireland, I sent Loretta Lynn the only fan mail I have ever written in my life. I wrote and told her how much her music meant to me. And I recall finishing off the letter with a line that went something like, 'Whenever you are feeling down, I just want you to remember that there are thousands of people like me who have a friendly kind of love for you.' Little did I know then that our paths were to cross a year later. Fate was about to smile on Daniel yet again, because Loretta had been lined up to appear on my show. God, I have an awful lot of favours to pay off. A lot is expected of the man who is given a lot.

The day Loretta Lynn was due into Ireland, you would think to look at me that it was my wedding day. 'Mr Cool' had suddenly lost his composure. I was up at the break of dawn, hopping around the place like a hen on a hot griddle. I was totally flustered. I couldn't sit down and relax. I had to keep on the move to occupy my mind. Isn't it amazing the influence that one individual can have over another? I know there are people who will tell me that that is how I affect them. I find the way I react to Loretta quite incredible, just as I am always surprised by the reaction of people to me. My itinerary for the day included a trip to Dublin Airport to greet Loretta personally and welcome her to the country. But when the time arrived for me to go out in the car, I got cold feet. I lost my nerve. I just couldn't summon up the courage to go out and meet the woman that I was absolutely devoted to. I made some excuse and got out of the trip. My friends will be surprised by this, because I normally take things in my stride.

But I wasn't off the hook. Like it or not, the moment would arrive when I would have no other option but to meet Loretta. Worse still, I had to sing with her and interview her during the show. While I was thrilled at the prospect of that, I was also terrified that I might go to pieces. Some time earlier, I had been told a story about an Irish photographer who was commissioned to photograph Johnny Cash and one of our own country singers, Sandy Kelly, when the two performed together in Ireland. Sandy's manager Kieran Cavanagh, who booked the photographer, didn't realise that the snapsman was a lifetime fan of Johnny Cash. When the moment finally arrived for the arranged picture to be taken backstage after a show and Johnny Cash walked into the room, the photographer fainted in front of his eyes. It was too much for the poor man, meeting his idol in the flesh. There was no photograph taken that night. I had an awful vision of something like that happening to me as soon as I found myself in the presence of Loretta.

I was up at the crack of dawn again the following day because it was the day that the show was due to be recorded. There was no breakfast for me that morning either – sure I wouldn't have been able to keep it down. While I was in my dressingroom at the TV studios, the sound of that wonderful voice drifted in. It was Loretta next door in her dressingroom. Well, I was like something that had been wrapped in tinfoil all my life and had been just opened up. My tummy was going into spasms. My legs hadn't the power to carry my body next door to say 'Hi.' People were telling me that Loretta had arrived, so I had to pretend that I was busy doing something while I tried to gather my wits. There was a walkman on the dressing-table, so I put on the ear-phones and pretended I was listening to it. Afterwards, I discovered that there wasn't even a tape in the machine!

Eventually, I made the supreme effort and walked next door to her dressingroom. You'd think I was going to the electric chair to look at me. Loretta was everything I had imagined her to be ... and more. She was a stunning-looking woman, with piercing blue eyes, Cherokee cheekbones and hair the colour of glowing coals. She gave me a big hug, and I felt I was going to die. I had the feeling of being in the presence of someone special. And Loretta is someone special. My rise to stardom from humble beginnings pales into insignificance in comparison with Loretta's achievements. She grew up in Butchers Hollow, Kentucky, dirt-poor and isolated. She was married at thirteen, a mother at fourteen and by eighteen she had four of her six children. By the time she reached thirty, Loretta was a grandmother. At thirty-two, she was a millionaire. And it is said she has had a tough time with her husband, Doolittle as she calls him, who early on succumbed to the demon booze and was also a womaniser. The story of her incredible life is chronicled in the film, *Coalminer's Daughter*. My mother had been to see the film and during Loretta and Doolittle's visit to Ireland for my show, she cornered Doolittle. 'You were a right boyo,' my mother told Doolittle, putting the fear of God into him. The poor man thought his time had come. She can be a very formidable lady, my mother.

Loretta Lynn has been a great inspiration to artistes like myself. What she has achieved without an education and despite being a child-bride and penniless, has given other performers hope and drive to strive for our goals. It was a great privilege to perform with Loretta and to be given the opportunity to speak with her. I relaxed once we started working together in the studio and the interview went very well. But, do you know, to this day I would be still too shy to approach her again if I met her. I would never go up to her and say, 'Hi, do you remember me? I'm Daniel O'Donnell, you were on my show in Dublin.' I could never do that. I would remain in the background if she walked into the room. She still has that kind of effect on me. I do intend to go and see her perform live in concert whenever I get the opportunity. But I don't plan to meet her. I would still be as shy and nervous as the first time we met in Wembley.

Cliff Richard is another artiste whom I admire greatly. And I have the same problem with Cliff as I have with Loretta. I find it very strange, particularly as I'm in the business myself, but I lose my nerve whenever I get close to a performer that I admire. It happened to me with Cliff. I went back to see him after one of his Dublin shows and when I met him I just didn't know what to say. I could hear myself babbling on about nothing. And I was telling myself: Shut up, what are you talking about? I don't know what Cliff made of me at all. I have tremendous respect for him. He conducts himself very well. He states himself excellently. The poor guy has got knocked more times than skittles, but he doesn't allow criticism to affect the way he performs or conducts his life. I could certainly do worse than take a leaf out of his book.

THOUSANDS FOR TEA

Wherever I travel around the globe, I never miss the opportunity to paint a picture of my own wonderful part of the world, County Donegal and its breath-taking beauty. It's my haven. It's my retreat. That's where I disappear to after a long concert tour to recharge my batteries. I return to my roots to walk the hills or fill my lungs with the pure sea air. Coming back from a long stint on tour, the magnificent view of the Donegal landscape immediately rejuvenates me. And I'll never lose my grip on reality once I maintain that contact with the place and the people who helped to make me the type of person I am today. It's not that I have any fear of my personality ever changing, but my family, neighbours and friends from my early days around Kincasslagh will ensure that I keep my feet firmly on the ground. It's great to go back there and just be plain Daniel Bosco 'from up the road'. Just like the old days when I was a youngster growing up there, I can saunter up the road and drop in unexpectedly on the neighbours for tea and biscuits. We chat about old times and it's rarely that the subject of my career will occupy the main thrust of the conversation. The people up in that neck of the woods are not the type to be impressed by stardom. I know they're proud that one of their own has achieved so much, and it doesn't have to be stated.

Of all the awards that I've received – I'm lucky enough to have received many – the one I treasure the most is the trophy that marks my selection as 'Donegal Person Of The Year' in 1989. That was a tremendous honour for me because it came from the people and the county that I hold dear to my heart.

The citation read: 'Daniel O'Donnell is a perfect example to the youth of our county and country. Success has not gone to his head. He has never forgotten his roots. He has not forgotten his mother and his family. He has not forgotten his beloved Kincasslagh and Donegal. And, above all, he has not forgotten the people who have put him where he is today – his loyal fans. He is never too busy to stay behind after shows to talk to them and sign autographs. Many are the stories that could be told of his visits to homes and hospitals to visit sick fans, even when this meant interrupting busy schedules. One story which aptly displays his concern for his fans is the one which tells of an occasion when it came to his notice that some fans who were itinerants were being refused admittance to his show. He refused to go on stage until they were admitted. Daniel never loses an opportunity to lend his name and his services, if possible, to worthwhile charities. A non-drinker and non-smoker, his clean-cut image in his dress and in his living standards does not meet with approval from some of the gurus in the media, who seem to wish he were otherwise. But they meet with the approval of us here in Cumann Tir Chonaill (County Donegal).'

The people who select the Donegal Person Of The Year felt that I was a great ambassador for the county on my travels and in my videos. The 'Thoughts Of Home' video includes many scenes of picturesque Donegal. But it's not that I've decided I'm going to do the job of the Irish tourist board. It's just that I'm so proud of my county that I want all my fans to come and see it. And to come and see Kincasslagh where I grew up.

During my concert tours I regularly tell audiences that if they're ever in Kincasslagh they're welcome to drop in for a cup of tea and a biscuit. I'm a great man for drinking tea. Now, as you know, I'm rarely at home in Kincasslagh, I'm usually off on tour around Britain and Ireland. Or else I'm in my new home outside Dublin. So, I'm not there to put on the kettle and entertain people if they decide to visit. And they do call all the time. They come over on holiday and track down my home. It must be the most photographed council house in Ireland at this stage. They knock on the door to see if Daniel is at home, and, of course, it's seldom that they strike it lucky. It's a wonder that my sister, Kathleen, and her husband, John, who live there with their young family, and my mother, haven't strung me up. It's lucky that they were always used to dealing with unexpected visitors. And they handle the situation very well. If I'm not there, my mother is the next best thing for the fans. And I think that she secretly enjoys all the attention. She certainly never hesitates to pose for a photograph.

The town of Dungloe, which is a short run by car from Kincasslagh, has an annual festival called the 'Mary From Dungloe', which has been running since 1968. It's a great excuse for a full week of partying and in recent years it has been attracting crowds of fifty thousand or more into the area. It's like the 'Rose Of Tralee', with girls representing many countries taking part in the 'Mary' contest. There is week-long dancing to top Irish bands and there's street music and everything else that goes with summer festivals of that ilk. I love being part of the whole event and I usually do a number of shows in Dungloe that week. In the months leading up to it, I remind fans right across Britain and elsewhere that I'll be at home during that week if they wish to call and see me. And I always nominate a day that they are guaranteed to meet me. In 1992, a total of three thousand people queued for hours along a narrow, rural road leading to my home. I was flabbergasted. I couldn't comprehend why people would queue for up to five hours to see ME. After all, I'm not in Loretta Lynn's league. But that's exactly what happened. My sister, Kathleen, and her merry band of helpers were busy that day dishing out the cups of tea! It's okay, she's still talking to me.

Some members of the Irish media who turned up to witness the strange event in a remote part of Ireland at the end of July, later commented that it looked like the type of scene you might expect to find outside the home of a faith healer. Well, I'm no faith healer. I have no powers like that. And nobody asked me for a cure. They just wanted to shake my hand, have a quick chat and, in most cases, a souvenir photograph of the brief meeting. But I was overwhelmed by the number who came to see me. They came from the thirty-two counties of Ireland. They were there from England, Scotland and Wales. And there was even a lady who travelled over from the Falklands.

I suppose fans like to catch me in my natural environment. They normally see me on stage when I'm Daniel O'Donnell – The Performer. The 'open day' at my home gave them the opportunity to judge me away from the spotlight. I wasn't dressed the way they'd normally see me during a performance. I didn't even shave on the day. The saw me in a relaxed home atmosphere. A wonderful aspect of the day, which is now an annual event, was that all the people there met new people. I encountered Catholics and Protestants from Northern Ireland who were travelling together and that is great. It's wonderful to see that there are no barriers when it comes to music and entertainment. That people can be united through their common love of song and dance. My own neighbours around Kincasslagh dropped in and mingled with the visitors and I was pleased with that. Sometimes I feel guilty about the numbers I attract into the area. I often wonder if I have interrupted the private lives of the locals and opened this remote part of the world to something that should not have been. But I don't think so. I think the people from my native Kincasslagh will never be swayed by anyone who arrives, but those who come will definitely be swayed by the local people. I believe that the people I grew up with have strong character and as long as they remain like that, the outside world will not affect them.

Without the people who called to my home during the 'Mary' festival, or the people who come along to my concerts and buy my records, Daniel O'Donnell – The Performer would not exist. And I don't know what I would have done if my singing career hadn't worked for me. So, I feel I owe all those people a debt of gratitude. They have given me all this success. They are responsible for all the good things in life that come with success. They have made me a very happy and fulfilled person, playing a role in life that I have never considered to be a job. Yet, the fans seem to think that they owe ME something. They shower me with gifts on tours and even the people who called to my home brought some beautiful presents and flowers. I could have set up a florist's shop in the village after they left that day. They really spoil me. On tour, I get everything from gold chains, bracelets and rings, to roses, teddy bears, tea bags and apple tarts. If I know that a person who gave me a particular item of jewellery is going to be at a specific show, I try to wear it for him or her to show my appreciation.

Their devotion to me is just incredible. I recall reading one story about a woman from Northern Ireland who has set up a mini shrine to me in her home. She has every tape I ever made and all the videos. And she has a scrapbook full of stuff about me. And mugs and cups I've drunk from. She said that when she's eventually called to meet the good Lord, she plans to be interred with one hundred photographs, wall charts and calendars of me, plus a flower I gave her, which she has pressed and preserved, and a bow-tie that I wore on stage. The story claimed she has given strict instructions to that effect to her bemused minister and family!

A question I'm often asked is, 'Why, unlike other performers, do you stay on for hours after a concert meeting the people who go to your shows? Is it not a terrible ordeal for you?' I can only smile at such a suggestion. What many people in show-business can't understand is that meeting the fans after a concert is one of the most satisfying aspects of my career. It's not gruelling for me. On the contrary, it helps me to wind down and relax after a couple of hours on the stage. Because I don't drink, I have no interest in rushing off to the bar or to a trendy nightclub. That's not my style. I love people. I love being with them. And I think that that can be attributed to my roots in Donegal. The fact that everyone around my area as a child ran an open house and there was a lot of interaction between neighbours. Naturally, because I meet so many people at the one time, I don't get to know a large number of them very well. But there are some that I'm very familiar with because I would see them at four or five shows (and in some cases nearly every show) during the same tour. There are people who travel hundreds of miles to my shows. I'm sure some of them clock up thousands of miles following me every year. I'm very fortunate to possess a really sharp memory, so I can recall a lot of people when I meet them again.

But if you ask me what it is about me that can command such devotion, I wouldn't be able to tell you. I don't dwell on it. I don't question it. I have never tried to analyse it. I'm just happy that there are people out there who like what I do and the way that I do it.

So, who are the fans? And what do they think of me? The Irish journalist, Eddie Rowley, who has worked with me on this book, spoke to some of the visitors who called to my home in Kincasslagh during the 'open day' on 30 July 1992. This is what they told him:

SHEILA DALZELLE - CUMBRIA

I had a very serious car accident back in 1985. It left me semi-disabled and unable to work. My world had collapsed around me. Then I discovered Daniel and life took on a whole new meaning again. I was always very fond of Irish music and I used to have tapes sent over to me from Ireland. One day a tape of Daniel O'Donnell arrived and from then on there was no one but Daniel for me. His music is very soothing and I got a lot of comfort from it. And, to me, Daniel was a bonus when I first met him. He was so nice and so friendly. He has filled in a big gap in my life. He has helped me to do things that I don't think I would have had the courage to do otherwise. I wouldn't have travelled long distances on a bus or train, for instance. But Daniel gave me the courage and motivation to do that because I knew he was going to be at the other end. Now I go on the bus down to London, which is a long way from where I live. Before that, I hadn't the confidence to travel. So, I have gained a lot of strength just from knowing Daniel and his music. He has visited me at my home and I just think that Daniel is everything that is right. Whenever I'm feeling down, I put on one of Daniel's videos, pull up a chair to the television and then I'm oblivious to everything around me. Daniel has helped me to accept what has gone wrong in my life. I had always wanted to take a trip on Concorde. So, in 1989, when I finally made up my mind to do it, I took Daniel to dinner on Concorde! And we had a ball. It was my way of saying thanks for everything he has done for me.

ROSE ORRIS - WALTHAM ABBEY, ESSEX, ENGLAND

I first heard Daniel O'Donnell's music on Radio 2 in England and I immediately fell in love with it. My youngest boy bought me one of Daniel's videos for Mother's Day. Daniel was marvellous in it, so I went out and bought all his tapes and videos. Then I joined his Fan Club and found out where all his concerts were on. Now, my husband, Tony, and I go to as many of his concerts as we can. We often travel two hundred miles on public transport just for one show. But it's worth it because he's such an exciting performer and he gives us so much pleasure. We are both totally hooked on his music now. This is our very first trip to Ireland and we travelled all the way over by car, even though my husband only started driving three weeks ago! We wanted to see Daniel in Ireland and nothing would stop us. My son, Stephen, did a lovely portrait of Daniel, which we have framed and we have given it to Daniel as a present for his new home.

THORA ALAZIA - THE FALKLANDS

I heard Daniel O'Donnell's music for the first time just after the conflict and I thought it was wonderful. I immediately joined his Fan Club and I got all his cassettes. He has a lovely voice and his music is beautiful. All my walls are now plastered with Daniel's pictures. He's very pleasant on the eye. And I have travelled over eight thousand miles to Ireland to see him. Everywhere you go in the Falklands, you hear Daniel's music being played. People are going to be really envious when I tell them that I've met Daniel. Daniel is all that I ever thought he would be ... and more. He's such a friendly young man. I'll never forget this visit to Ireland, even if I never get back again. It will be the one thing that I'll always carry with me.

ANNE RONAN - SEDBURY, CHEPSTOW, GWENT, WALES

I started going to see Daniel O'Donnell in concert in 1987 and he was such an exciting performer. He brought me so much joy. Later, when I was diagnosed as having multiple sclerosis, Daniel was very kind and very caring to me. And we have become great friends. Even though I'm incapacitated, I follow him everywhere. I have wonderful friends who take me to his shows all over Britain. On his last tour, I saw eighteen of his twenty-five shows. I follow him to Scotland, England, Wales, Cornwall, Ireland – he's my whole life now. One day, I saw a van pulling up outside my home. I couldn't believe my eyes. It was Daniel. He was on his way to a concert in Cardiff and he called to see me. That day will never be taken out of my life. He said, 'Where's the tea, Anne?' I kept saying, 'I can't believe you're here!' He made his own tea, bless his heart. We had a little chat and off he trotted. I don't think I'll ever forget it. That's the kind of person Daniel is. People don't realise what he does behind the scenes. He has a heart of gold.

MY TEAM AND ON THE ROAD

The Daniel O'Donnell show is by no means a one-man-band. I would never have achieved so much without the back-up of an outstanding team of people. Showbiz is a breeding ground for the cynical, the opportunist and the ruthless. But I have been very lucky with the calibre of the people who work with me. I'm surrounded by people who are good for me and people I'm happy with, both on and off the stage. There is no one who gives me any hassle. And there is not a single individual in the organisation that I'm not comfortable with. And that's very important. If you're not getting on with the people you work with, then you cannot function to the best of your ability. But who are the key people? What's their background? How did I team up with them?

MICK CLERKIN - *HEAD OF RITZ*

The man who made it all happen for me. Mick Clerkin is The King. He definitely has the Midas touch. His first big success was way back in 1981/1982 with The Fureys. They had a major hit with 'Sweet Sixteen', which sold a quarter of a million copies. After finding the winning formula, Mick's next successful outing in Britain was with Foster and Allen and their hit, 'A Bunch Of Thyme'. By that stage, people were beginning to sit up and take notice of Mick Clerkin. Irish artistes suddenly saw him as a stepping stone to the top in Britain. Mick's own success as a businessman was not achieved overnight. The affable man from Ballyjamesduff, County Cavan, came up the hard way, serving his apprenticeship when he started as road manager with Larry Cunningham and The

Mighty Avons in 1966, after they had a hit with 'Tribute To Jim Reeves'. When Larry Cunningham decided to leave The Mighty Avons, he asked Mick to become his personal manager. Mick was at first reluctant to take on the daunting task, fearing that he wouldn't be able to do it justice. But Larry obviously recognised Mick's potential way back then and persuaded the County Cavan man to launch a new career. His very first venture as a manager was a tour of the States, which was a big success for Larry Cunningham.

Mick told me how his real love was always the record industry. He later cut his teeth in the business in a Dublin-based company called Release Records. Mick always believed that there was a viable market for middle-of-the-road (MOR) music in Britain. It just needed to be developed. The record company he owned at the time had a massive Irish hit with 'One Day At A Time'. It was released by an Irish singer called Gloria. Mick then approached four major record companies in Britain with the single. But after listening to the first verse and chorus, they all said: 'Thank you very much. Not for Britain.' Mick still believed it had potential in Britain, but he had no outlet there at that time. But a couple of months later, the seed was sown for the emergence of Ritz when an American singer, Lena Martell, released 'One Day At A Time' in the UK and it turned out to be the only million-record seller that year.

The opportunity to have a crack at the British MOR market came along with 'Sweet Sixteen', which was a big hit in Ireland for The Fureys. Their manager, Jim Hand, gave Mick the go-ahead to promote it in Britain. Mick and a partner, the late Peter Dempsey, went over to London and set up their operation in the London Ryan Hotel, after securing a special rate. They worked out of there for three months. Terry Wogan was on the radio in those days and he was a big asset. Terry was always a good man for playing Irish releases if the quality was good. He thought 'Sweet Sixteen' was a magical record and played it on air. It was a massive hit and Mick was on his way with Ritz. BBC Radio 2 in Britain, which has a big influence on record sales, began to support Ritz as a label that came up with good quality MOR releases.

Despite its success, Ritz is quite a small company. And I believe that is one of the secrets of its success. Mick's policy is to keep the number of artistes on his label down to a minimum. By doing that, Mick ensures that each artiste – and we are all different – gets individual attention and adequate resources. Ritz also has a concert division, managed by company director Eamon Leahy.

They started promoting Foster and Allen initially. Now they promote all my concerts and I doubt if any other promoter could have achieved the same level of success for me. Ritz have a very good relationship with regional radio stations around Britain, which most promoters would not have the same contact with. A gentleman called Paddy McIntyre has a full-time job keeping in touch with all the radio stations, which are invaluable in spreading the news about my concert appearances. I don't think I would be at the level I now enjoy in Britain if it wasn't for the backing of the radio stations. They have been very, very helpful. The Ritz company is comprised of people who believe in what they are doing and are enthusiastic about the artistes they are promoting. When they go to work on promoting a singer, the staff pull out all the stops. If they have to work from nine o'clock in the morning till ten o'clock that night to achieve something, then they'll do it. You wouldn't get that kind of commitment from people who took on the job merely because it was a job.

SEAN REILLY - *MY MANAGER*

I have already documented my feelings for Sean Reilly. A native of Kilnaleck, County Cavan, Sean started his working life in a number of jobs. He was a barman for a short time. He worked in a furniture factory. And he was a car salesman. Like Mick Clerkin, he was always friendly with the band members in Larry Cunningham's group, The Mighty Avons. And he got to know their road manager, Mick Clerkin. When Mick went into the record company business, Sean joined him in 1968, working as a roadie with a group called Gary Street and the Fairways. He then progressed to managing that band. For most of his career, Sean was manager to the highly regarded Irish country singer and songwriter, Ray Lynam and his group, The Hillbillies. Now he's managing a young fella by the name of Daniel O'Donnell and a lovely female country singer, Mary Duff.

I have a great band behind me, which is a tremendous asset to any artiste. We get on very well together. The fans also love them and each individual has his own following. It's not unusual at shows to see people coming up with gifts for the lads, as well as for myself.

BILLY BURGOYNE - *DRUMS*

A native of Ballinasloe, County Galway, Billy Burgoyne is the man I mostly rely on. He's the band leader and whenever I have anything to discuss or anything I'm not happy with, I go to Billy. Prior to joining me, Billy worked with The Hillbillies for twelve years and he spent five years with a pop band called Jukebox. Billy made one of his earliest appearances with me as a session musician on the album, *Two Sides Of Daniel O'Donnell*.

RONNIE KENNEDY - *ACCORDION/KEYBOARDS*

Ronnie Kennedy is the band member I'm closest to. If there's tension, Ronnie and I will bring it out in each other. We go back a long way and on stage we have a great rapport. A native of the Dublin suburb of Ballyfermot, he was a founder member of my original band, The Grassroots, which lasted two years. Prior to that, he worked with Johnny McEvoy for fourteen years.

TONY MURRAY - *BASS GUITAR*

Tony Murray from Athlone, County Westmeath, has been with me since the launch of my current band. Before going into music full-time, Tony was a jack-of-all-trades. He worked in a record shop at one stage. And he was a barman. Tony was a member of Jukebox for two years after deciding to become a professional musician.

JOHN STAUNTON - *RHYTHM GUITAR*

John Staunton is a native of Ballintubber, County Roscommon. He performed with me on my first recording session and has worked with a number of local bands in Ireland, including T.R. Dallas, with whom he spent a total of seven years.

BILLY CONDON - FIDDLE

An all-round musician whose experience ranges from *céilí* music to orchestral, Billy Condon initially trained as a teacher. Moving onto music, he started out as a classical musician before joining the Irish traditional group, Napper Tandy. He was also a member of Ray Lynam's Hillbillies for eleven years.

RICHARD NELSON - *STEEL GUITAR*

A native of Ahoghill near Ballymena, County Antrim, Richard Nelson replaced Kevin Sheerin in 1992. Prior to that, Richard worked as a session musician in Belfast and Dublin and was a member of a number of bands, including Mary Duff and Logue and McCool.

RAYMOND M^cLOUGHLIN - *PIANO*

The youngest member of the band, Raymond McLoughlin has taken over from John Ryan, who left the group in 1992. Raymond was born and reared in London. His parents are natives of Swinford, County Mayo. He joined my band straight out of college.

The other members of the team who travel on the road with me, include Loretta Flynn, Jim Rosie and Joe Collum. Loretta is well known to the fans, being the secretary of my Fan Club. She's also my personal assistant on tour. I first met Loretta when she started coming to my shows back in 1984/1985, with her sister and cousin. We struck up a friendship and Loretta, who is a native of Waterford, took over the running of the Fan Club with her sister, Breda, operating out of the Ritz office. It was always more than a working relationship. We were good friends. And occasionally she would travel with me to concerts. She would give me cups of tea while I prepared for a show backstage. She started looking after my clothes. Eventually, it reached the stage when she was travelling with me all the time and looking after me. As my workload built up, I found that I needed someone to look after the organisation of my stage gear on a full-time basis. So Loretta fitted the bill. She plays a very important role in my career, because it's Loretta who liaises with the fans. She meets them during shows and takes requests, messages and so on. It's obviously not possible for me to meet everyone, so Loretta plays a key role in keeping me in touch with the people who follow me.

When my career started to grow and grow, people used to say to me, 'Oh, you'll soon have minders.' I used to laugh it off. But now I do have a guy called Joe Collum from Ballybofey

County Donegal, who plays that kind of role in my set-up. When I'm not working, I look after myself. I go wherever I want to go. And I don't need anyone to travel with me or to organise anything for me. But when I'm on tour it's a little different. Joe is always on hand to ensure that things don't get out of control. He's also my driver when I'm on the road. Jim Rosie from the Orkney Islands off the coast of Scotland, is the compere and he's also a crowd organiser.

The days of the band travelling together in the back of a van are now behind us. Nowadays, we don't live in each other's pockets, and I think that helps us to maintain a good working relationship. We travel in different cars to shows these days. I usually travel with Joe, Loretta and Jim.

I'm always a little nervous on the day of a show. After all these years and despite the success I've enjoyed, the nerves have never left me. I'm usually quite fidgety. I walk around, lift things up and put them back down, and they wouldn't look any better when I'd put them back. And I usually have to visit the loo numerous times. When I'm on tour, my day usually doesn't start until about 12 noon, because, depending on the distance we travel, it may be 3 a.m. to 4 a.m. before I would get to bed. I normally have a cup of tea and a biscuit before leaving the hotel. Then we set off to the next destination. I like to eat my main meal before 4 p.m. And I only have one substantial meal a day. I like plain food, steak or scampi, and I love chicken Kiev (I don't get many kisses that night, thanks to the garlic!). At night, I would normally have a sandwich. Sometimes, as a special treat after a concert in England, I like nothing better than to stop at a service station late at night and have a feed of chips, sausages, beans and bacon. Delicious! I very often stop at Watford Gap, because I got to know some of the people there early in my career. When I'm in London, I

Our neighbour Annie McGarvey at the old forge, Kincasslagh. Dear Annie has always been a major [ ] my life. Below: Thousands for tea! The scene outside my home in Kincasslagh on a summer's day in [ ] hen 3,000 people turned up to meet me.

Right: Getting into the swing of things on stage at The Dome during the Mary From Dungloe festival in County Donegal, July 1992. Below: Meeting the fans outside my home in Kincasslagh.

the helm. Taking over the controls on the boat to Arranmore island where I perform every year.

Above: Over 6,000 people turned up for my Welcome Back show at Dublin's Point Theatre on 11 July 1992. It was a night to remember.

Above: My band [1992]: Ray McLoughlin, John Staunton, Billy Condon, me, Tony Murray and Richard Nelson. Front: Billy Burgoyne and Ronnie Kennedy.

sometimes get a kebab late at night and take it back to my friend Joan Tobin's where I stay. Then I put chips between the pitta bread and dip it in tomato ketchup. Gorgeous! But I try not to do that kind of thing too often because it doesn't do the waistline any good.

From about two o'clock in the afternoon before a show, I start getting my voice warmed up for the performance. The shows usually kick off around 7.30 p.m. and end around 10.15 p.m. Then I'm back out chatting with the fans within half-an-hour. Every day is the same. Very routine and very organised. That is, with the exception of the night at Middlesborough when there was a bomb scare and the police evacuated the theatre. We were all herded out on to the street. And as we waited for the all-clear, I mingled with the crowd and got chatting with the fans. One woman told me how she had come to hear me sing her favourite song, 'The Old Rugged Cross'. So I decided to sing it there and then for her on the street. The police then came along and suggested that it would be safer if we all made our way up to the local park. That's exactly what we all did. And I got up on a park bench and sang another couple of songs. Then the police turned up again and this time they offered me the use of the loudspeaker in their panda car. I took them up on their offer and sang another few songs through their loudhailer. A strange night, that one!

WALKING ON WATER

The media has portrayed me as 'Mr Perfect', the boring boy next-door. Whiter than white. Never puts a foot wrong. Never a bad word to say about anyone or anything. A real goody-goody. A real drip! Maybe I am boring by their standards. I probably don't make good 'copy' for them. There are no sex-and-drugs scandals. No paternity suits. I'm not drying out in some famous clinic. I don't sleep in an oxygen tent. I haven't had a 'face lift' or any other kind of cosmetic surgery. Well, not yet, anyway. I suppose I am quite conservative in a lot of ways. I'm very traditional in the way that I lead my life, clinging onto the values that were instilled in me by my mother, teachers and the clergy. I do practise my religion, which is Roman Catholic. I'm very close to my family and to the neighbours in Kincasslagh. I don't ever want to lose contact with my background. And I suppose I lead a very normal existence, as normal as I can in this strange world of showbusiness. So, taking into account the bizarre images that are often associated with showbiz figures, the tag 'Mr Perfect' or 'Mr Boring' does fit the character in my case. But they couldn't be further from the truth. I am, after all, only human. I don't walk on water. Well, I've never tried!

There are people who put me up on a pedestal. They seem to think that I'm some kind of saintly figure and that I don't have faults like they do – that what they do, I would never do. But I'm really no different to anyone else. I have my bad moments, the same as the next person. If people stayed around long enough, they would hear me letting out the odd swear word. I have a wicked sense of humour at times, and like many others I can sometimes see the funny side of another person's misfortune. There are moments when I have a short fuse. And when my temper blows, I have a wild, sharp tongue. There would be no answer to what I might say. And in those circumstances, I'm not always right. Nobody is right all the time. It's usually the people I think most of that I lose my temper with. People in the band. Family. Friends. You always hurt the ones you love. It would be instantaneous. And then it would be all forgotten just as quickly. I suppose that comes as a surprise to most of my fans. They would be devastated if I lost my temper with them. They would feel that they were cut in two and that they'd never heal. It's not that I have a dreadful temper. But I do have a sharp tongue.

I have developed a 'hard neck' since entering this business. I needed to in order to survive. I am the recipient of some very strong emotions from the general public. There are some people who love me with a passion that is almost frightening. But there is another section of society that despises me with the same intensity of feeling. And, sadly, I have to say that I'm only referring to Ireland in this case. I am aware that people outside my own country who have read the other references in this book to the slating I have been subjected to throughout my life, are bemused by this revelation. I don't have to suffer insulting remarks or jibes in the street when I'm abroad. But I do when I'm at home. I love Ireland and I love Dublin, as well as Donegal, and I won't let anything or anyone stop me doing what I want to do when I'm at home. I enjoy going into the city centre of Dublin and I do whenever I get the opportunity. But, invariably I am at the receiving end of a barrage of jeering remarks from gangs when I'm out and about there.

I obviously hear the sneering because my tormentors usually shout their comments after me. Sometimes I answer them.

Sometimes I don't. The times I answer normally ends up in an argument, which I never win. Of course the comments hurt me. And it's something I shouldn't have to live with in Ireland, because I've done nothing wrong. What have I done to deserve it, except, perhaps, get up their nose? But if they don't like me as a singer, then they don't have to listen to my songs. It's that simple, really. Just switch off the radio or change the station. My image is not doing them any harm. There is no need to abuse me on the street or in other public places. I can take it because I've got used to it. But, unfortunately, it often occurs when I'm out with friends or members of my family. And that is really unfair. When the Irish Olympic boxing champions Michael Carruth and Wayne McCullough returned from Barcelona in August 1992, I went out to Dublin Airport to join the crowds for the big homecoming celebrations. I had my young nephews with me, and again, I was the target for a few guys in the crowd. That was embarrassing. And it only happens when people are in a group. Individuals don't slate me. I wonder do those people feel foolish when they think about it later?

A whole industry of Daniel O'Donnell jokes has also developed in Ireland. The night I travelled to Dublin Airport to share in the joy and happiness generated by the return of the young boxers, a guy in the crowd actually tried to tell me one of them. Can you believe that? It's a strange feeling being at the end of jokes. But I do have a sense of humour. And I can laugh at them, provided they're not malicious. I've heard the one that goes, 'Did you hear that Daniel O'Donnell got a girl into trouble? He told her mother she was smoking.' And during the Gulf War there was a joke about Saddam Hussein planning to pull out of Kuwait on the Friday because I was doing a concert there on the Saturday. The night I performed at Dublin's Gaiety

Theatre, the war was still raging. I was hoping that Saddam would have gone by then because I had planned to tell the audience: I don't know what I'm going to do for the next couple of weeks because I was going to Kuwait for a concert!

I have my own way of coping with the hassle I get when I'm out and about in Dublin or elsewhere in Ireland. I look down a lot of the time when I'm walking the streets. I avoid eye-contact with people. But I don't mind speaking to people when they speak to me. But when people in groups start to taunt me I just keep walking at a fast pace without showing any emotion. Then they're never really sure whether it's me or not. Because I'm well known, some people feel I should surround myself with minders. But I don't have any worries at all about myself in that respect. I've never been mobbed. I don't think I ever will be. It would be awful if it happened. I do everything that I want to do. I go everywhere that I want to go.

While I may be a superstar to people while I'm performing, once the spotlight goes out and I leave the stage, my lifestyle is very normal. I'm sure there are lots of people outside showbusiness who lead more exciting lives. You won't find me at glitzy parties. You won't see me tripping the light fantastic in trendy nightclubs. I don't go to the top restaurants to eat. I don't tear around in a flashy Ferrari car. That word 'boring' is probably creeping up on me again. The things that interest me are very ordinary. My social life in the eyes of the world is very boring, but it's wonderful to me. I love going into Barry's Hotel in Dublin to dance. It takes me back to my early days in the city when dances like those in Barry's were all the rage. I referred to them earlier in the book. The likes of The Irish Club and The Ierne, where I danced every night of the week. I've never been the sporting type. My only form of recreation has always been dancing. Once I get going, I never leave the floor all night. And the bands I danced to years ago are still around today. The legends of the ballroom era are still with us. People like my favourite Irish singer, Philomena Begley. Barry's Hotel is preserving the atmosphere and the entertainment of a by-gone era in Ireland and for as long as it continues, you're likely to find me there raising the dust on the dancefloor.

I don't take much interest in current affairs. And I take little or no interest in politics. It's something I can't understand about myself. But I was never interested in current affairs. I generally don't even bother buying a daily newspaper. I am concerned about the situation in the Third World. My ambition used to be that one day I would go and work in the missions. But I don't know if I'll get the opportunity now. And I would love to see peace in Ireland. I often wonder is there anything I can do to help heal the rift in Northern Ireland. I look at my audience and I see how Catholics and Protestants can come together and be united through their love of music and entertainment. And I wonder if there's a Protestant person in public life that I could team up with to help in some way. But I suppose that's very idealistic from my point of view.

I've been a pilgrim to St Patrick's Purgatory in Lough Derg, near Pettigo, County Donegal, a number of times. It's a windswept island where people go to do penance, usually when they're seeking some kind of favour, or in thanksgiving for a favour, or to atone for their sins. Back in the fifth century, Saint Patrick is said to have gone there on a pilgrimage to pray that the pains of Purgatory be revealed to him. His request was granted and he then ordered that the island should become a place of pilgrimage for sinners. I must be a terrible sinner, having been there so many times! I started doing the pilgrimage in 1979 to pray that I would pass my exams. Whenever I did it, I was always asking for something or saying thanks for something. You spend three days on the island, fasting and praying and there's a one-day vigil without sleep. As soon as you get there you remove your footwear and you remain barefoot for the entire period on the island, as you do the stations of the cross walking on sharp rocks and cold stone floors. For me, the significance of it is that everyone is equal there. Everybody is reduced to the same level. Regardless of what you have on the outside, you don't have it on that island. It's a great leveller. I always found the experience rewarding, but it gets more difficult every time.

I love live music. And I'm a great fan of the Irish bands, the veterans and the newcomers, who play the style of music that I like. When I'm not working myself, I go to venues all over Ireland to see other singers perform. I think the up-and-coming performers at home are very talented and very entertaining and it's great to see new talent emerging because they're the life-blood of the live entertainment scene. I like to go and hear other bands and then go home immediately afterwards. I'm not interested in going anywhere else after Barry's. I'm not interested in going to receptions that I get invited to. I feel I would be uncomfortable with the people there. I don't even know where the trendy nightclubs are located in Dublin. I don't know if I'll ever visit them. I don't plan to at this time.

My other big passion is playing a card game called 'whist'. It's run on an organised level all over the country. They call the games 'whist drives'. In recent times, I've been playing all over County Kildare, as I now live on the Dublin-Kildare border. I play in places like Naas and Prosperous. It's a very popular game in my native Donegal, so that's where I picked up the basics as a teenager. I used to be one of the 'hot' players in Kincasslagh. But the Kildare air mustn't be agreeing with me because I didn't get much of a run at the games there. One night I won the 'booby' prize, which was £2 and a pack of cards for the longest sitting. I think they were trying to tell me something with the pack of cards. 'Go home and practise.' But it's a very relaxing game. And the people I play with have no connection whatsoever with showbusiness. So there's no showbiz talk, which is great. I can totally unwind.

I'm a big sun worshipper and I enjoy sun holidays. I try to snatch a week or two in a foreign sun spot whenever my work schedule permits. Cyprus is my favourite destination. The people are really friendly there. They have a wonderful climate, with sunshine eleven months of the year. And the food is delicious. I always return with a really deep tan and I think that is due to the fact that my mother comes from an island and islanders are usually very dark. There's nothing I like better than lazing around in the sun. And believe it or not, I have something in common with the pop singer, Michael Jackson – I love amusement playgrounds. I have never lost that child-like fascination with fun rides and the big wheel and the other amazing attractions that are available nowadays. In January, 1992, I went to Disneyland in Florida and took along all my young nephews and nieces. I don't know who had the most fun. The kids or 'Uncle Daniel'. I didn't feel so foolish meeting Mickey Mouse when I had the youngsters with me. And my passion for the delights of Disney didn't end there. Later in 1992 I took off for a few days to EuroDisney in France with fellow Irish singer Sean O'Farrell, and we had a ball.

For a guy who professes to enjoy the beauty and serenity of Donegal, you'll probably be surprised to learn that I also love the 'jungle' that is New York. I have been to the 'Big Apple' on holiday several times and it fascinates me. I'm a great people-watcher, as I have already mentioned, and I could stand for hours observing the colourful characters on the streets of Manhattan. Mind you, that's probably not a very safe hobby to be practising there. I remember the first time I took a bus into Manhattan from John F. Kennedy Airport. The driver's parting words to me were: 'Don't let anyone help you with your bags. Don't let anyone get you a taxi. Give no-one money. Welcome to New York.' It was a strange introduction to a city. The 'city that never sleeps' sure is life in the fast lane.

My best friend at home in Donegal is still P.J. Sweeney. He works in The Cope and plays in a local band at night. We have been friends since schooldays, but our friendship was firmly established when we went off on a foreign holiday together one time. Time spent with somebody tends to make or break a friendship, and P.J. and I got on very well together on that holiday. We went to the Greek island of Crete and had a wonderful time – we never stopped laughing. I remember one night we were out enjoying the entertainment and we noticed two ladies throwing shapes on the dancefloor. We decided to join them. We weren't interested in going out with them, we just wanted to have some fun, so we joined them on the dancefloor and pretended we were foreigners and couldn't speak English. We danced with them several nights after that, maintaining our pose as 'foreigners.' Then one day we met them on the street and P.J. forgot himself and said, 'How's it goin'?' Strangely enough, they carried on a conversation with us without any reference to our act! Then P.J. and I hired out a little scooter and that was hilarious. He's over six feet tall and weighs about fifteen stone – well, the poor little scooter was huffing and puffing trying to go up a hill. I had to get off because it didn't have the power to carry the two of us. It was a great carefree holiday that I'll always remember.

Lost Love

Like most people, I've been through the wringer in the love stakes. And I still have a mountain to climb when it comes to establishing a personal relationship, because there is no one in my life at present. But there have been several girls who set my heartbeat racing at various stages. I have fallen victim to the love 'sickness' that strikes when Cupid's arrow picks you out as a target. Cupid has a lot to answer for. The palpitations you experience whenever you set eyes on the object of your desires. The butterflies in your tummy that kill your appetite and make your mother think you're ailing, and should she call a doctor? The all-consuming passion in the first flush of love that makes you lose interest in everything else. Cupid must have a great laugh, watching the effects of that little arrow.

The first love of my life came along when I was only a wee lad in national school. A little girl arrived in our area on holidays, and, God, she was the most beautiful little girl I had ever laid eyes on. I suppose I was curious about her because she was a stranger. She was exotic to me because she came from the outside. To this day, I don't even know what part of the country or the world she was from. At secondary school, there were also a couple of girls with whom I had a brief and innocent attachment. I was always very secretive about them because I didn't want my mother to know. I probably felt that she would frown on me getting involved with a girl at that early stage of my life and try to put a stop to it. I went out with one girl at school for a good while. I used to meet her in Dungloe and we'd go out for walks. And we'd meet at dances too. It was all very harmless in those days. Nowadays, they're jawin' [kissing] as soon as they meet on a dancefloor.

Looking back, I never had a serious romance in my teenage years. Cupid only went to work on me in earnest when I joined Margaret's band. That little arrow found me the day we booked into a London hotel. There I was, minding my own business, when whoosh!, the arrow found me. She worked in the hotel and the moment I saw her, I was smitten. I was on cloud nine. All I could think about was her. It was a wild sensation to be so infatuated. I would have walked on water for her. But what happened? She ditched me and went off with someone else. But that was the time I could have made the biggest mistake of my life. I would have gone all the way and married her if she had stayed with me. I was mad about her. But I was only twenty-one, and I know now it wouldn't have lasted jig-time. I was too young. I don't think fellas are as mature at twenty-one as their female counterparts. I was also earning very little money and I wouldn't have been able to support a cat, never mind a family. And had I married at that stage, I doubt that I would have been able to launch a solo career. I think a lot of people make the mistake of marrying young. Their mind is telling them: This is heaven; this is where it's at and this is how I'm going to be happy. But, unfortunately, it doesn't always work out that way. Nevertheless, I was shattered when she rejected me. I've been devastated by the break-up of several romances. But I'm a funny individual. As soon as something is over, I just pick up the pieces immediately and get on with life.

But that guy with the bow and arrow still had an interest in me, and shortly after the break-up of that romance, I met a girl with whom I have had the most special and most important relationship that I have ever had, and maybe will ever have. We were together for eight years and it ended in the beginning of 1992. I am not going to go into the details because that would be unfair to her. I'm not even going to mention her name or the names of any of the other girls I've been involved with. I think if I revealed any of the intimate details of any of my relationships it would be a betrayal. They are private people who are not in the public eye.

But if there's anything I've lost out on in life, it's love. And that's because I've always put my career first. Until now I haven't been prepared to put the same commitment into my personal life as I have devoted to my career. I have lost out on love, but I wouldn't be without the music. Maybe I'm selfish. And maybe I'm ruthless. But there was nothing, and I mean NOTHING, that was going to keep me from achieving what I wanted to achieve. It's nothing to do with finance. It's to do with being successful. It's to do with being a singer. I had an incredible drive. I still have, obviously, otherwise I would never have succeeded. The drive may not be as apparent now as it was, but I still have it. I still want to be the best. And everything else is secondary.

Being so caught up in your career, you can end up becoming oblivious to the needs of those close to you. They need just as much of your attention, but you don't see that because you're so busy. You can take a lot for granted. The fact that you can't be with a person so much, because of the commitments that your work demands. What you don't take into account is the fact that it's not their career. It's not their work. The person close to you doesn't always, if ever, get the same satisfaction or the same enjoyment out of your achievements and your success. They are a part of your life, not because of your career, but because they are in love with you as a person. You have to be around to nurture and develop a relationship, and it's always very painful when you lose a person who has been part of your life for so long.

Now, I'm not lonely. I suppose I'm a little sad. But I don't feel the need to be with somebody. I suppose if I did, the career would not have been as important. It might be hard for people to understand that. But that's how I feel right now. I also feel that it's very difficult for me to get to know somebody now. At this stage, I find it very hard to ask somebody out. I think, in an ideal situation, I would like to meet somebody who would not be aware of who I am or what I do for a living. And then, when they like me for myself they can find out the rest. But that will probably never happen. So, I suppose it's a case of wait and see what will happen. But, if and when the time comes that I meet somebody I want to share my life with, I will have to change. I know that. I'll have to change. I'll have to be less determined career-wise. My career takes up a lot of my time, particularly at night. I've never been the type of guy who would go to a dance to pick up a girl for a 'one-night-stand'. I never did that. I was never into casual relationships. I never set out to pick up a girl for what I might get from her sexually. But then, despite what others might say, I think a lot of people are like that. When I was in my 'teens, fellas always gave the impression that they were very sexually active with girls they had picked up on a casual basis. But I firmly believe that it was a lot of bravado. There was no foundation for half the wild stories that were told. That was never my form. And it's certainly not my style nowadays.

Although I don't have a girlfriend to share my life at present, I have a very special female friend, Josephine, in whom I confide all my innermost feelings and conflicts. I suppose, in a way, Josephine is a surrogate girlfriend. But our relationship is not a physical one. It's purely platonic. Josephine is married and has her own family life, but I could never spend enough time with her because she brings me such joy. She's my confidante. She's my psychologist. She's my rock. Josephine makes me happy. She's a good listener and she doesn't tell me any lies. She's up with me when I'm up. She's still up when I'm down.

I first met Josephine in 1973, when I was only eleven years old. She was a friend of my sister, Margaret. Josephine and a group of her friends were fans of Margaret and used to regularly attend her shows all over the country. That's where I made contact with Josephine and over the years we have become soul mates. She's the best thing that ever happened to me, along with Sean Reilly. She's better than the music. Better than all the success. I think people will find that difficult to understand. It is impossible to measure just how much Josephine means to my life. It's an unbelievable relationship to have with someone. It's worth a fortune. Josephine now lives just ten minutes down the road from my home outside Dublin. So she's close-by whenever I need her. I'm very lucky because I don't think everybody has that kind of relationship with another human being. As soon as Josephine walks through the door, I come alive. So, God has been good to me.

OUT OF CONTROL

The year 1992 was a very strange year for me. It was a very uncertain year. It was a year when I discovered more about myself than I did in the past ten. And it started on 1 January, with a dramatic phonecall to my manager, Sean Reilly. During a brief conversation, I said to him, 'Sean, I'm worried about my voice. I need to speak to you.' He immediately said, 'Come over.' And I knew before I left what I was going to do. I had decided to go off the road. The one thing I didn't need was for anyone to go against me – what I mean is that it was going to be easier if nobody went against me. I went into Sean and told him I needed to take a break. He asked, 'How long?', and I said it would probably be about six months. I had decided that following the advice of my voice specialist, Tom Wilson.

As I have said earlier, of all the people that I could have teamed up with management-wise, I'm very lucky to have found Sean Reilly. There's a great human element to Sean. His immediate response to my decision to put my career on ice for six months was, 'That's fine. Leave it with me.' There was no haggling over the amount of time I was planning to take off. No pressure from Sean to fulfil the concert dates that I was already committed to and for which a large number of tickets had been sold. Sean's only concern was for my welfare. That's the calibre of the man I have as my manager. He's a rare species in the showbiz world and, believe me, I don't take him for granted.

I left Sean that day with a sense of relief. A burden had been lifted from my shoulders, because I knew I couldn't do it anymore. But there was also the awful realisation that it was all over for me. Although, I've always said I knew I was going to come back, I have to admit now that for a while I really thought it was the end.

In the short period of six years, I had made an incredible leap forward in the showbiz world. From being virtually unknown and struggling to secure dates even in my own country, I had reached a stage where I was a major concert attraction in Britain and Ireland, with my albums and videos selling hundreds of thousands of copies. But you don't achieve that level of success without paying some kind of price. And I almost paid the ultimate. I was physically exhausted.

My thirtieth birthday on 12 December 1991, was one of the worst days of my life. I did a concert in Letterkenny, County Donegal. It should have been super, but my throat was sore, I was exhausted, I just couldn't cope with it. People will probably be shocked to discover that I was feeling that way. I was very near to total exhaustion. I suppose the signs had been there for a long time. I had been irritable. I mentioned earlier about having a short fuse and at times I would blow up with members of the band or other people on the road with me. When I look back, I realise now that the pressure was getting to me. I knew that there was something wrong with me. I felt it in The Galtymore in London's Cricklewood in the middle of my British tour. I had it on 12 December. I definitely had it in The Beaten Path, Claremorris, County Mayo, on 26 December. And I don't ever want to experience that kind of exhaustion again. I had to cancel a show the night after The Beaten Path. I wasn't able to sing. I wasn't able to talk. When I woke up on the morning of 29 December, I was still exhausted. And I had a show ahead of me that night in the Cush Inn, Kildangan, County Kildare. I decided to go ahead with it. But during the performance I knew that every song I sang was getting closer to the one that was going to be the last.

I told the audience that night when I went on stage at The Cush Inn that I had a sore throat, that I didn't know how long I was going to sing for. Then later on that night, after I had been on for about an hour, it was very near stopping time. Eventually, I wasn't able to sing anymore. It was the strangest sensation. I had pushed myself too much. I was all things to everybody and nothing to myself. When I took a break during the show, I asked my personal assistant Joe Collum to ring Sean and ask him to cancel everything that was coming up before our planned holiday on 6 January. I went back on stage and told the audience a couple of jokes. I didn't sing very much after that because with the passing minutes my throat got progressively worse and eventually it wasn't working at all. I don't know if the audience were aware of how I was feeling because I was always very good at concealing my form. But they gave me a standing ovation as I left the stage.

I was very lucky that I stopped when I did. It was either stop the bus or go around the corner and crash. I knew that around the corner I was going to crash. I was my own worst enemy. There was nobody at any time driving me too hard. Why did I feel I had to do so much? Because so much was put to me. When you get a letter from somebody who's a lot worse off than you — I don't mean financially — it's very hard to turn around and say, 'Well, I can't do anything about that.' I had been thinking about stopping for some time before I did. But I used to think: How can I stop? The majority of the people in the band are married. What are they going to do? What about all the concerts that are sold out? And so on. But that line of thinking is ludicrous and stupid, because if you are no good to yourself, you are no good to anybody. And that's what I realised at the end of December.

In early January 1992, I went off on a pre-arranged holiday to Orlando, Florida, taking my young nephews and nieces to Disneyland. While I was relaxing down there, news reached me from home that there were some strange stories circulating about my health, the most grotesque being that I had throat cancer and would never sing again. Looking back, my pre-planned holiday was a blessing in disguise. I avoided all the fuss surrounding my 'illness'. The newspapers were full of it. And poor old Sean was inundated with queries from journalists. There was even a story in showbiz circles that I had orchestrated the whole saga so that I could get rid of my band without having to sack them. Needless to say, all those stories were without foundation. When I arrived back at Dublin Airport after a gruelling flight, during which I thought we were all going to die because the turbulence was so severe, there were even media people waiting for me at Arrivals. I had never experienced that before in Ireland. Sickness is obviously bigger news than singing.

Back home, I now had time to take stock of my situation. I felt a terrible emptiness as the full impact of what had just happened to me began to sink in. I had been on top of the world. But now the rug had been pulled from under my feet and I was in 'no man's land'. My voice had gone. My career had gone, at least temporarily. I felt at that time that my purpose in life had gone. I didn't even have a home. Before Christmas 1991, I sold my house on the southside of Dublin city. I was in the process of buying another residence on the Dublin-Kildare border. But the deal hadn't gone through. So, I now found myself in a rented apartment in Dublin. Alone, and in strange surroundings, I was really feeling sorry for myself. I was like a fish out of water. I had never really been out of work. Even though times were hard in the beginning, the drive to succeed was always there to motivate me. Now it seemed that all that had changed.

During the days and weeks that followed, I came to terms with my new lifestyle and set about the task of rebuilding my physical strength again. I started working out in a gym to get back into shape – and I hated every minute of it. Despite my best efforts, I never got close to giving Arnold Schwarzenegger a fright. I started doing all the things I never got the opportunity to do when I was working. Things like going to the theatre, dancing, and playing whist and ten-pin bowling. I went along to see other singers perform. And I was contributing my weekly column to the Irish Sunday newspaper, *Sunday World*. Did you know I was a part-time journalist? And I've done a bit of radio broadcasting in my day. Maybe that's where I'll eventually end up! So, a routine gradually began to develop. My days were starting earlier. Instead of getting out of bed in the afternoon, as I do when I'm working, I started getting up around the same time as everyone else.

For about a year before I had to finally throw in the towel, I was attending a Dublin throat specialist, Tom Wilson. I had never been formally trained as a singer. So Tom took me back through the basics. He taught me how to sing from the diaphragm and not just the larynx. I'm not saying he has turned me into a Pavarotti or a Carreras. I'm neither of those and I never will be. I haven't got the perfect technique for singing and I still get a little hoarse from time to time when I sing. But I don't get as hoarse as I used to and I can sing above it. So, Tom played a big role in getting me back on the stage again.

But physically, I was still feeling dreadful. I kept saying to people, 'I have something wrong with me!' I went to doctors. They carried out all kinds of tests on me. 'Nothing wrong. Nothing wrong,' they told me. But I insisted that there was a tightness in my chest. I blew into every tube there was to blow into, but they couldn't find anything. Eventually, I went to a herbalist, Sean Boylan. He discovered that my diaphragm was out of position. He stretched me and I could hear the crack as he rectified the problem. Then he gave me herbal medicine, which I really feel has helped me a lot, too.

I feel better now. And when I talk to people, I feel that I'm a joyful person again.

Conquering the Mountain

When my career was in jeopardy, I coped with the trauma by turning to God. As I have said I believe I'm run-of-the-mill where religion is concerned. I'm not obsessive about it. It has always been important to me, but I don't consider myself to be over-religious. But during those dark days when I faced an uncertain future, I started to seek solace through my faith. And I began to think: Well maybe there's something else HE wants me to do. Maybe there's another area I need to discover about myself. I mention that during my shows nowadays when I tell the audience how I'm very pleased HE didn't want me to do something else.

During the early stages of my recuperation, I had decided that I would be able to return to the stage earlier than had been initially anticipated. With the advice of Tom Wilson, I decided to start back on 1 April. But as that date drew near, I was filled with a sense of foreboding. A fear of the unknown began to consume me. And, physically, I didn't feel an awful lot better. I hadn't been attending the herbalist Sean Boylan for very long at that time. During the last couple of weeks before that first concert at The Civic Centre in Halifax, I experienced bouts of panic. I was very, very nervous.

On the big night, my system was in tatters. I wasn't functioning properly at all. I don't know how I got through that night. Waiting in the wings to go on, the power left my legs. And when it was time for me to step out, those legs refused to carry me to the middle of the stage. I had to lean on a speaker to support myself. But when I heard the sound of my voice, my confidence gradually began to build up. I got through the night.

After that, it was like climbing the ladder again. From then on, I progressed step by step.

One of the biggest concert venues in Ireland is The Point Theatre. It has played host to the big names in almost every category of music, from Carreras to Don Williams to U2. Early in 1992, my manager Sean Reilly and Irish country music promoter Kieran Cavanagh got together at Dublin's Mont Clare Hotel and hatched a plan for me to perform there on my 'comeback' in Ireland. When Sean told me about it, I was hesitant at first. The Point, to me, was beyond my wildest aspirations. My dreams never went as far as The Point. No other Irish country singer had ever performed there as the main attraction. People have often accused me of not taking risks, but this was certainly going into unknown territory. I have great faith in Sean and eventually I said, 'If you think I can do it, then let's do it.' I felt that because he was confident that I could do it, I should be confident that he could make it a success.

It takes a lot of people to fill Dublin's Point Theatre and I was apprehensive about how it would turn out. But Kieran Cavanagh is a professional and highly respected promoter. He's the man who brings many of the big American country acts into Ireland. Kieran and Sean spent several months planning the big concert for me. The promotion wasn't just concentrated on Ireland; fans who come to see me in Britain were also notified about it through hand-bills distributed at the various venues. Travel packages by sea and air were organised and advertised. The technical side of my show also had to be revamped. We had never played that size theatre before, so extra lighting and sound equipment was hired to ensure a proper impact.

The morning of Saturday, 11 July 1992, finally arrived and I was up at cockcrow. I couldn't sleep due to a combination of nerves and excitement. I remember thinking: 'Jeez, I wish I had gone out to a dance last night. I would have slept later.' Irish country singer Mick Flavin had been playing in Barry's Hotel the previous night, but I had resisted the temptation to go to that dance because I wanted to be bright and energetic for my own show. That day involved lots of trips to the loo. A big show is certainly a great cure for constipation! During the day I had a sound check, so that helped to pass away a couple of hours. The band was in great shape. I had prepared my programme for the show three weeks previously and they had done a number of eight-hour days rehearsing it under the charge of my musical director, John Ryan. When he felt he had them at their peak, I was brought in. So, everything was sounding good for later that night.

It was a relief to discover on the night that there were over six thousand people in the theatre. Now it was up to me to do the rest. As the overture was playing before I went out on stage, a wave of emotion swept through me. I think it was the realisation of just how far I had come in Ireland. Playing to a full house at The Point Theatre was the pinnacle of my career at home. It was a big moment for me. So, I suppose I savoured that a little as I prepared to step out on the stage. But as soon as I appeared in front of the crowd, those feelings left me. As I was singing 'The Rose Of Tralee', I felt a great sense of pride that, at long last, so many Irish songs were being sung in The Point. The audience that night was wonderful. They were like a choir and I could hear them singing all night. They knew all the songs, especially the slow numbers which they could really get into.

Looking back, I feel my show at The Point has helped to alter dramatically Irish people's image of me. I think I gained a lot of respect and admiration through my live performance that night. There were a lot of people at the show who had never seen me in action before, except on TV. They had absolutely no idea about the content of the show. They probably expected to be bored by a guy who they thought would stand in the one spot all night singing. But, as my regular concert-goers know, there is a lot of energy in my live act. Afterwards, one woman said to me, 'I've never seen you before', and I don't know if she was asking me, Why?, or asking herself, Why? And I suppose that is the nicest compliment anyone can give me. A lot of people remarked on how I was leaping into the air and putting on a physically demanding performance. Many were surprised by the rock 'n' roll aspect of it, where I do a medley of Elvis hits, including 'That's Alright Mama', 'Love Me Tender', 'Are You Lonesome Tonight' and 'Don't Be Cruel'. That's good for me because it's another form of expression and it's important for me to show people that there's more to me than just a white suit and a clean-cut image. There are also a lot of young people who come to see me and they like to see that kind of action.

The people who don't realise that I do have a sense of humour were surprised to hear me telling jokes and giving the odd bum-wiggle during my performance. But a show is made up of lots of elements and you lift people in different ways. With the songs. With the music. With the way you express yourself when you're speaking. And with your body movements. I'm not trying to give the impression that I'm Tom Jones, although I did have a bra thrown at me during the show at The Point. It was the first time that that ever happened to me and I must admit it was a bit of a shock. The lady in question had put her name and address on the inside with a message asking me to send her a card. I duly obliged. On stage, I'm very different. I'm much more outgoing and I'm much more assertive. There's a part of me for the stage that never comes out anywhere else. I'm totally at home and I feel I'm very confident when I'm up there.

What I'm doing mightn't be everybody's cup of tea and I know it isn't. But if you come along and see my show, I hope you will find that I do it on a very professional level and to the best of my ability. And if I feel it's going to do them any good, I will sometimes take other singers up on stage to perform at my shows. People often ask me why I do that. But it doesn't do me any harm to have new talent coming on the scene. I can only perform in one venue on any one night. There's plenty of room for everybody, plenty of success to go around.

On reflection, my concert at Dublin's Point Theatre marked the beginning of a new era for me. My break from the scene allowed me to take a long hard look at my career. And I realised that I could no longer continue giving so much of myself, both on and off the stage. Physically, it's just not possible to do it, as I discovered. I realise now that I pushed myself to the limit trying to do everything that was put to me. The pressure eventually brought me to my knees. If I was a drinker, I probably would have ended up an alcoholic. If I was into drugs, I hate to think what the consequences might have been. But I didn't have a crutch like that. And because I didn't have a crutch, I was standing straight all the time. At the end, I was just high enough to see over the cloud to say that: 'This is awful. I need to clear this area.' I don't really know how long I had to clear it. But I believe now that I didn't have very long. I also held it all in. I tried not to show people just how tired I was feeling. And I suppose that takes more out of yourself, trying to give the impression that you're up when you're not up at all.

The pressure I brought upon myself was a result of the close contact I have with people. Because I'm very accessible I'm asked to do a lot of things outside of showbiz. There are numerous requests for private visits and I have always said, 'Sure, no problem.' I'm not saying I was some kind of Samaritan running to people every day of the week. But I did a lot of that behind the scenes. Now, it's very hard for me to go and visit people and then do a show. It wasn't in the beginning. And that's what I couldn't understand. I was asking myself, 'Why am I so tired when I was actually doing more in the beginning?' When I look at my first year with Ritz, I was out morning, noon and night. But I wouldn't be physically capable of doing that now. I feel I have learned how to cope with a career at this level. I think I'm fairly well adjusted. In the early days, I had no time for myself. It wasn't healthy. That's something I've had to rectify. But I still don't want to be locked away. I still want to meet people. That's important to me too. I have reorganised my show so that I don't spend as much time on stage as I used to. Consequently, I feel my live performance is much better now because I don't become exhausted. I'm certainly getting more enjoyment out of my concerts and the shows are attracting a wider range of people.

When I look at my life, I have enjoyed more than I thought I would ever have had the opportunity to do. But luckiest of all is that success didn't smother me. It almost did, but I feel I'm now better adjusted for this life than I used to be, as a result of that experience. And whatever comes my way from now on will be a bonus. And who knows what will happen – sure, I'm only thirty!

DISCOGRAPHY
Daniel O'Donnell Single Releases

TITLE	TRACKS
Summertime In Ireland	Summertime In Ireland
	My Side Of The Road
	Take Good Care Of Her
	I Wonder Where You Are Tonight
Two's Company	Two's Company
	Home Sweet Home
	Violet And The Rose
	The Streets Of Baltimore
Far Far From Home	Far Far From Home
	My Shoes Keep Walking Back To You
	Home Is Where The Heart Is
	Shutters And Boards
Last Waltz Of The Evening	Last Waltz Of The Evening
	You Know I Still Love You
Marianne	Marianne
	A Country Boy Like Me
Letter From The Postman's Bag	Letter From The Postman's Bag
	A Loved One's Goodbye
The Three Bells	The Three Bells
	Silent Night
	An Old Christmas Card
I Just Want To Dance With You	I Just Want To Dance With You
	Rockin' Alone
	My Irish Country Home

Daniel O'Donnell Albums

TITLE

TRACKS

THE BOY FROM DONEGAL

Donegal Shore
The Old Rustic Bridge
Galway Bay
Forty Shades Of Green
My Side Of the Road
5,000 Miles From Sligo
The Old Bog Road
Slievenamon
Noreen Bawn
Ballyhoe
Home Is Where The Heart Is*
Shutters And Boards*

THE TWO SIDES OF
DANIEL O'DONNELL

The Green Glens Of Antrim
The Blue Hills Of Breffni
Any Tipperary Town
The Latchyco
Home Town On The Foyle
These Are My Mountains
My Donegal Shore
Crying My Heart Out Over You
My Old Pal
Our House Is A Home
Your Old Love Letters
21 Years
Highway 40 Blues
I Wouldn't Change You If I Could

I NEED YOU

I Need You
Sing An Old Irish Song
From A Jack To A King
Lovely Rose Of Clare
Stand Beside Me
Irish Eyes

I NEED YOU (cont'd)	Dear Old Galway Town
	Three Leaf Shamrock
	Veil Of White Lace
	Kickin' Each Other's Hearts Around
	Medals For Mothers
	Wedding Bells
	Snowflake
	Your Friendly Irish Way
	Lough Melvin's Rocky Shore
	I Love You Because
DON'T FORGET TO REMEMBER	Don't Forget To Remember
	I Don't Care
	Old Loves Never Die
	I Wonder Where You Are Tonight
	Don't Be Angry
	Roses Are Red
	Before I'm Over You
	Take Good Care Of Her
	Pretty Little Girl From Omagh
	Green Willow
	Don't Let Me Cross Over
	The Good Old Days
	Pat Murphy's Meadow
	I Just Can't Make It On My Own
FROM THE HEART	The Minute You're Gone
	It Doesn't Matter Anymore
	Mary From Dungloe
	Bye Bye Love
	The Old Rugged Cross
	Wasting My TIme
	Kelly
	Things
	Act Naturally
	Honey
	Wooden Heart
	It Keeps RIght On A'Hurtin'
	My Bonnie Maureen

FROM THE HEART (Cont'd)

I Know That You Know
Old Dungarvan Oak
Danny Boy

THOUGHTS OF HOME

My Shoes Keep Walking Back To You
Mountains Of Mourne
London Leaves
Blue Eyes Crying In The Rain
Old Days Remembered
Send Me The Pillow You Dream On
Moonlight And Roses
A Little Piece of Heaven
Far Far From Home
Isle Of Innisfree
My Heart Skips A Beat
I Know One
I'll Take You Home Again Kathleen
Second Fiddle
My Favourite Memory
Forty Shades Of Green

FAVOURITES

Bed Of Roses
Forever You'll Be Mine
Excuse Me (I Think I've Got
  A Heartache)
Halo of Gold
The Streets Of Baltimore
Geisha Girl
Life To Go
That's A Sad Affair
Bringing Mary Home
Home Sweet Home
The Banks of My Own Lovely Lee
Home Is Where The Heart Is
Dublin In The Rare Ould Times
The Green Hills Of Sligo

THE LAST WALTZ

Here I Am In Love Again
We Could
Last Waltz Of The Evening
When Only The Sky Was Blue
Heaven With You
You Know I Still Love You
Talk Back Trembling Lips
The Shelter of Your Eyes
When We Get Together
Ring Of Gold
A Fool Such As I
Memory Number One
Look Both Ways
Little Patch Of Blue
Marianne*

THE VERY BEST OF
DANIEL O'DONNELL

I Need You
Never Ending Song Of Love
Don't Forget To Remember
A Country Boy Like Me
She's No Angel
Stand Beside Me
Eileen
Pretty Little Girl From Omagh
Danny Boy
The Wedding Song
My Donegal Shore
Letter From The Postman's Bag
The Three Bells
Our House Is A Home
A Loved One's Goodbye
Home Is Where The Heart Is
The Old Rugged Cross
You Send Me Your Love
Take Good Care Of Her
Standing Room Only

(track marked * appears on compact disc only)

Other Books from O'Brien Press

Irish Rock
Mark Prendergast
A comprehensive account of twenty-five years of Irish music.

The Stunt
Shay Healy
A wild novel set in the music world.

West Cork Walks and Kerry Walks
Kevin Corcoran
For the active, great walks through Ireland's wild and beautiful places.

The Haughey File
Stephen Collins
The amazing Haughey career by a well known journalist.

Simplex Crosswords – Books 1-3
Popular series from *The Irish Times* for the crossword lover.

Smokey Hollow
Bob Quinn
Growing up in Dublin in the forties and fifties. Hilarious!

Land of My Cradle Days and The Changing Years
Martin Morrissey
Life in Ireland before electricity and with the old farming methods.

For a complete list (including children's books) write to the O'Brien Press or consult your bookseller.

THE O'BRIEN PRESS
20 Victoria Road, Dublin 6, Ireland.